YOUR recipe could appear in our next cookbook!

Share your tried & true family favorites with us instantly at

www.gooseberrypatch.com

If you'd rather jot 'em down by hand, just mail this form to...

Gooseberry Patch • Cookbooks – Call for Recipes
PO Box 812 • Columbus, OH 43216-0812

If your recipe is selected for a book, you'll receive a FREE copy!

Please share only your original recipes or those that you have made your own over the years.

Recipe Name:

Number of Servings:

Any fond memories about this recipe? Special touches you like to add or handy shortcuts?

Ingredients (include specific measurements):

Instructions (continue on back if needed):

Special Code: **cookbookspage**

Over ➤

Extra space for recipe if needed:

Tell us about yourself...

Your complete contact information is needed so that we can send you your FREE cookbook, if your recipe is published. Phone numbers and email addresses are kept private and will only be used if we have questions about your recipe.

Name:

Address:

City: State: Zip:

Email:

Daytime Phone:

Thank you! Vickie & Jo Ann

Busy-Day
SLOW COOKING

Gooseberry Patch

An imprint of Globe Pequot
246 Goose Lane
Guilford, CT 06437

www.gooseberrypatch.com

1•800•854•6673

Copyright 2016, Gooseberry Patch 978-1-62093-187-5

Do you have a tried & true recipe...

tip, craft or memory that you'd like to see featured in a **Gooseberry Patch** cookbook? Visit our website at **www.gooseberrypatch.com** and follow the easy steps to submit your favorite family recipe. Or send them to us at:

Gooseberry Patch
PO Box 812
Columbus, OH 43216-0812

Don't forget to include the number of servings your recipe makes, plus your name, address, phone number and email address. If we select your recipe, your name will appear right along with it... and you'll receive a **FREE** copy of the book!

Table of CONTENTS

DEDICATION

To everyone who likes shortcuts in the kitchen...more time to spend with family & friends!

APPRECIATION

A big "Thanks" to all of our friends who shared their very best slow-cooker recipes with us.

Warm & Cozy

BREAKFASTS

Cheddar Cheese Strata

Kelly Alderson
Erie, PA

My favorite egg recipe for late-morning brunches. Sometimes we enjoy it as breakfast-for-dinner too.

3 c. milk
14 slices white bread, torn and
    divided
3 c. shredded sharp Cheddar
    cheese, divided

1/4 c. butter, diced and divided
6 eggs, beaten
2 T. Worcestershire sauce
1/2 t. salt
paprika to taste

Warm milk in a saucepan over low heat just until bubbles form; remove from heat. In a well-greased slow cooker, layer half each of bread, cheese and butter; set aside. In a bowl, whisk together warm milk and remaining ingredients except paprika. Pour into slow cooker; sprinkle with paprika. Cover and cook on low setting for 4 to 6 hours, until set. Makes 6 to 8 servings.

A simple fruit salad goes well with brunch dishes. Cut seasonal fruit into bite-size pieces and toss with a simple dressing made of equal parts honey and lemon juice. Add a sprinkle of poppy seed or chopped fresh mint.

Family-Favorite Potatoes

Shelley Turner
Boise, ID

*Packed with bacon and cheese, these potatoes are our favorite
for weekend breakfasts. We love them at dinnertime too.*

4 russet potatoes, peeled, cubed
   and divided
1/4 c. onion, chopped and
   divided
salt and pepper to taste

2 T. butter, diced and divided
6 slices bacon, crisply cooked,
   crumbled and divided
1 c. shredded Cheddar cheese,
   divided

In a lightly greased slow cooker, layer half each of potatoes and onion;
season with salt and pepper. Add half each of remaining ingredients.
Repeat layering, ending with cheese. Cover and cook on low setting
for 8 to 10 hours, until potatoes are tender. Serves 4 to 6.

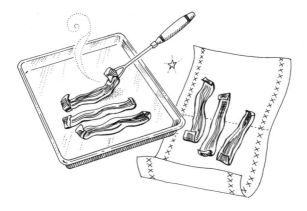

Prepare crispy bacon easily in the oven. Place bacon slices
on a broiler pan, place the pan in the oven and turn the temperature
to 400 degrees. Bake for 12 to 15 minutes,
turn bacon over and bake for another 8 to 10 minutes.

Crustless Broccoli Quiche

JoAnn

This is a very versatile recipe...in springtime I like to use asparagus instead of broccoli. It's a great way to use up leftover shredded cheeses you may have in the fridge.

6 eggs
2 T. all-purpose flour
1/2 t. salt
pepper to taste
1/8 t. nutmeg
1 c. half-and-half
1 c. whole milk

3 c. cooked broccoli or other vegetable, chopped and well-drained
2 T. fresh basil, minced
1 c. shredded Gruyère cheese
1 c. shredded Parmesan cheese, divided

In a bowl, beat eggs with flour and seasonings; whisk in half-and-half and milk. Stir in broccoli, basil, Gruyère cheese and 1/2 cup Parmesan cheese. Pour egg mixture into a well-greased large slow cooker. Sprinkle remaining Parmesan cheese on top. Cover and cook on high setting for 1-1/2 hours, or until just set in the center. To serve, run a knife around the edge of quiche; cut into wedges. Makes 6 servings.

Place a bunch of fresh herbs in the fridge in a water-filled tumbler, covered with a plastic bag. They will keep their just-picked flavor up to a week, ready to use in recipes.

Cheesy Southern Grits

Zoe Bennett
Columbia, SC

At our house, it wouldn't be breakfast without grits! We love them alongside scrambled eggs and crispy bacon.

1-1/2 c. stone-ground or regular
    long-cooking grits, uncooked
6 c. water
1 c. heavy cream
1-1/2 to 2 T. butter, softened

1 T. salt
Optional: small amount of milk
1 c. shredded sharp Cheddar
    cheese

In a slow cooker, combine all ingredients except optional milk and cheese. Cover and cook on low setting for 6 to 8 hours, stirring occasionally. If mixture starts to dry out, stir in a little milk. About 15 to 30 minutes before serving time, stir in cheese; cover and finish cooking. Makes 8 servings.

Hosting a game-day or holiday brunch? Use a slow cooker set on low to keep sausage gravy, scrambled eggs or other breakfast foods warm and toasty.

Breakfast Burritos

Connie Hilty
Pearland, TX

My teenage boys are always hungry, it seems! I love this recipe because it's so simple to fix and makes a lot. They love being able to grab a couple burritos, wrap them up and head for the schoolbus.

20-oz. pkg. refrigerated diced
   potatoes, divided
1/2 lb. bacon, crisply cooked,
   crumbled and divided
1/2 lb. ground pork breakfast
   sausage, browned, crumbled
   and divided
3 c. shredded Cheddar cheese,
   divided

1/2 c. green pepper, diced
1/2 c. onion, diced
1 doz. eggs
1 c. milk
1 t. salt
12 to 15 burrito-size flour
   tortillas
Garnish: salsa, additional
   shredded cheese

In a large slow cooker, layer half each of potatoes, bacon, sausage and cheese. Add all of green pepper and onion. Repeat layering, ending with cheese; set aside. In a large bowl, whisk together eggs, milk and salt; pour over layers in slow cooker. Cover and cook on low setting for 7 to 8 hours. To serve, spoon mixture into tortillas; garnish as desired and roll up. Makes 12 to 15 servings.

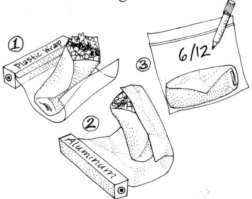

Make extra burritos and freeze them for an easy heat & eat meal later. Wrap each cooled burrito in plastic wrap, then in aluminum foil. Place wrapped burritos in a freezer-safe zipping bag marked with the date...so simple!

Mexican Breakfast Casserole

Rita Morgan
Pueblo, CO

I first tried this recipe when I was planning a church breakfast potluck...it was a hit! Now I serve it often.

9 taco-size corn tortillas, divided
1 red pepper, diced and divided
3/4 c. green onions, sliced and
   divided
8-oz. pkg. shredded Mexican-
   blend cheese, divided
1 lb. ground breakfast sausage,
   browned, drained and
   divided

8 eggs
1-1/2 c. milk
1 T. canned diced green chiles,
   drained
1 to 2 T. fresh cilantro, chopped
Garnish: salsa

Spray a large slow cooker well with non-stick vegetable spray. Arrange 3 tortillas to cover the bottom of slow cooker, tearing to fit as needed; set aside. Reserve 2 tablespoons red pepper, 2 tablespoons green onions and 3/4 cup cheese; refrigerate. To slow cooker, add half of sausage and half each of remaining red pepper, green onions and cheese. Add 3 more tortillas, torn to fit; repeat layers. Top with remaining tortillas, tearing as needed to cover mixture. In a large bowl, whisk together eggs, milk and chiles; pour mixture over top. Cover and cook on low setting for 4 to 5 hours, or on high setting for 2 to 3 hours, until set in the center. Top with reserved cheese, pepper and onions; add cilantro. Serve with salsa. Makes 6 to 8 servings.

Make sure to use the right-size slow cooker...they work best when at least half of the crock is filled.

11

Apple Coffee Cake

Pamela Elkin
Asheville, NC

I recently found this recipe in a box of old recipes of mine. It is covered with spattered signs of usage. Reading over it brought back memories of how delicious it is. It is wonderful for a holiday brunch!

5 T. butter, softened and divided
21-oz. can apple pie filling
3 T. light brown sugar, packed
1 t. cinnamon, divided
18-1/2 oz. pkg. yellow cake mix

2 eggs, beaten
1/2 c. sour cream
1/2 c. evaporated milk
Optional: 1/4 c. chopped pecans
Optional: whipped cream

Spread one tablespoon butter over bottom and sides of a 4-quart slow cooker. Combine pie filling, brown sugar and 1/2 teaspoon cinnamon in a bowl. Spread 1/2 of apple mixture in bottom of slow cooker; set aside. In a separate bowl, combine dry cake mix, eggs, sour cream, evaporated milk, remaining cinnamon and remaining butter; beat well. Spoon 1/2 of batter over apple mixture in slow cooker. Layer with remaining apple mixture; spoon remaining batter over filling. Sprinkle with pecans, if desired. Cover and cook on high setting for 2 to 2-1/2 hours. Turn off slow cooker; let cool for about 15 minutes. Serve topped with whipped cream, if desired. Makes 8 servings.

A weekend morning is the perfect time for a chat over coffee cake and coffee. Invite a girlfriend, or the new neighbor you've been wanting to get to know better, to share the latest news...you'll be so glad you did!

Overnight Blueberry French Toast   *Vickie*

Sweetly satisfying!

1 c. brown sugar, packed
1-1/4 t. cinnamon
1/4 c. butter, melted
12 slices white bread, divided
1-1/2 c. fresh or frozen
   blueberries

5 eggs
1-1/2 c. whole milk
1 t. vanilla extract
1/2 t. salt
Garnish: whipped cream,
   additional blueberries

Combine brown sugar, cinnamon and melted butter in a bowl; mix well. Sprinkle 1/3 of mixture evenly in the bottom of a greased slow cooker. Cover with 6 bread slices. Sprinkle with another 1/3 of brown sugar mixture. Spread blueberries on top. Cover with remaining bread slices. Sprinkle with remaining brown sugar mixture and set aside. In a large bowl, whisk together eggs, milk, vanilla and salt; pour evenly over top. Press down gently on bread slices with a spoon. Cover and refrigerate overnight. In the morning, place crock into the slow cooker. Cover and cook on low setting for 3 to 4 hours, until set and golden on top. Serve topped with a dollop of whipped cream and a few berries. Makes 6 to 8 servings.

Enjoy fresh blueberries throughout the year...just freeze them during berry season! Spread ripe berries in a single layer on a baking sheet and freeze until solid, then store them in plastic freezer bags. Later, pour out just the amount you need.

Mushroom & Cheese Strata

Angela Murphy
Tempe, AZ

A brunch favorite! I keep a bag in the freezer for extra slices of bread, then when I have enough, I treat the family.

1/2 lb. sliced mushrooms	8 eggs
1 T. olive oil	2-1/2 c. milk
5 c. day-old Italian or white bread, cut into 1-inch cubes and divided	2 T. fresh thyme, snipped
	1 T. Dijon mustard
	1/4 t. salt
2 c. shredded Swiss cheese, divided	pepper to taste

In a skillet over medium heat, sauté mushrooms in oil for about 5 minutes, until mushrooms are softened and liquid is evaporated. Spray a slow cooker generously with non-stick vegetable spray. Spread 1/3 of bread in slow cooker; spoon half of mushrooms over bread and top with 1/3 of cheese. Repeat layering with half of remaining bread, remaining mushrooms and half of remaining cheese. Top with remaining bread. In a large bowl, beat together eggs, milk, thyme, mustard, salt and pepper; pour over bread. Gently press down bread to absorb egg mixture. Sprinkle remaining cheese on top. Cover and cook on low setting for 7 to 8 hours. Uncover; let stand for 15 minutes before serving. Makes 8 servings.

Day-old bread is fine for making stratas, stuffing cubes and bread puddings. It keeps its texture better than very fresh bread...it's thrifty too!

Sausage & Egg Casserole

Patricia Wissler
Harrisburg, PA

*My children always loved having this casserole for breakfast
on Sunday mornings. We like the mustard, but you may
omit it if you prefer.*

1 to 2 T. butter, softened
14 thick slices white bread
2 t. mustard
1 lb. ground pork breakfast
    sausage, browned, drained
    and divided
2-1/2 c. shredded Cheddar
    or Monterey Jack cheese,
    divided

1 doz. eggs
2-1/4 c. milk
1/2 t. salt
1 t. pepper, or to taste

Spread butter generously in a slow cooker; set aside. Spread bread
slices with mustard on one side; cut bread into large squares. In slow
cooker, layer 1/3 each of bread pieces, sausage and cheese. Repeat
layering twice, ending with cheese on top. In a large bowl, beat
together eggs, milk, salt and pepper; pour over cheese. Cover and cook
on low setting for 8 to 9 hours, until set. Makes 6 hearty servings.

I have always been delighted at the prospect of a new day,
a fresh try, one more start with perhaps a bit of magic
waiting somewhere behind the morning.

- J.B. Priestley

Apple-Brown Sugar Oats

Tyson Ann Trecannelli
Gettysburg, PA

Even your picky eaters will love this one!

2 c. whole milk
1 c. long-cooking oats,
   uncooked
1 c. apple, peeled, cored and
   diced
1/2 c. raisins
1/4 c. brown sugar, packed

1 T. butter, melted
1/2 t. cinnamon
1/4 t. salt
Optional: 1/2 c. chopped walnuts
Garnish: light cream or
   additional milk

Spray a slow cooker with non-stick vegetable spray. Add all ingredients except garnish; stir to mix well. Cover and cook on low setting overnight, about 8 hours. Spoon oatmeal into bowls; top with cream or milk. Makes 6 servings.

Early risers will appreciate finding a slow cooker of overnight oatmeal awaiting them in the morning! Set out brown sugar and a small bottle of cream on ice so everyone can top their own.

Homemade Yogurt

Sonia Daily
Rochester, MI

Most store-bought yogurts have some added sugar, so I experimented and came up with this version of homemade yogurt. Whole milk and a bit of cream make a delicious treat that is great for low-carb dieters. Serve with fresh berries or just enjoy it plain.

1/2 gal. whole milk	6-oz. container plain yogurt,
1 c. whipping cream or	or 3/4 c. yogurt from a
half-and-half	previous batch

Pour milk and cream or half-and-half into a slow cooker. Cover and cook on low setting for 3 hours. Unplug slow cooker; let cool for 3 hours. Remove one cup of milk mixture from slow cooker to a bowl; stir in yogurt. Add mixture to slow cooker; whisk well. Add lid; wrap entire slow cooker with a blanket or towel. Let stand for 8 hours to overnight. Spoon yogurt into covered containers refrigerate. Makes 12 servings.

A healthy quick breakfast! Layer crunchy whole-grain cereal, juicy fresh berries and creamy low-fat yogurt in a parfait cup. Add a spoon and breakfast is served!

Holiday Hashbrowns & Ham

Gladys Kielar
Whitehouse, OH

Turn on your slow cooker for this recipe when you go to bed...
you'll have a delicious breakfast in the morning.

26-oz. pkg. frozen shredded
   hashbrowns, thawed
2-1/2 c. cooked ham, cubed
2-oz. jar chopped pimentos,
   drained

10-3/4 oz. can Cheddar
   cheese soup
3/4 c. half-and-half or milk
pepper to taste

Combine hashbrowns, ham and pimentos in a lightly greased slow cooker; set aside. Stir together remaining ingredients in a bowl; pour over hashbrown mixture. Cover and cook on low setting for 6 to 8 hours. Makes 8 servings.

A budget-friendly source for cooked ham...ask for the end cuts at the deli counter. Ends too small to return to the slicer are often sold at a reduced price. Just remove the casings and dice.

Bacon-Hashbrown Breakfast Casserole

Rebecca McKeich
Palm Beach Gardens, FL

Every Christmas morning, our whole extended family descends upon our house to see what Santa has brought. It is our tradition to eat breakfast before we dive under the tree. After a couple years of making breakfast from scratch for a large group first thing in the morning, I came up with this. Prep it beforehand, toss it in the slow cooker before bed and you've got breakfast ready when you wake up. Just add coffee!

26-oz. pkg. frozen shredded
    hashbrowns, thawed
1 lb. bacon, crisply cooked and
    crumbled
16-oz. pkg. shredded Cheddar
    cheese

1 doz. eggs
1 c. milk
1 T. dry mustard
salt and pepper to taste

Spray a slow cooker generously with non-stick vegetable spray. Spread hashbrowns evenly in bottom of slow cooker. Top with bacon and cheese; set aside. In a large bowl, whisk together eggs, milk, mustard, salt and pepper. Pour over top and spread evenly. Cover and cook on low setting for 6 to 8 hours, until set. Makes 8 servings.

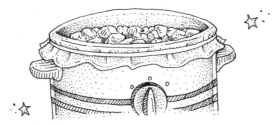

If a slow-cooker recipe calls for a spritz of non-stick
vegetable spray to the inside crock, try using a disposable
plastic slow-cooker liner instead...clean-up will be a breeze!

Old-Fashioned Baked Apples

*Marsha Baker
Pioneer, OH*

*I love these easy baked apples stuffed with cranberries or raisins...
real comfort food. The recipe is so versatile...sweeten with sugar,
sweetener or honey. I prefer Gala apples, but McIntosh, Rome or
Empire would be delicious too. This recipe will bring raves!*

4 to 6 Gala apples
1/3 c. water
6 to 9 T. dark brown sugar,
   packed
4 to 6 T. sweetened dried
   cranberries or raisins
2 to 3 t. cinnamon

allspice or nutmeg to taste
4 to 6 T. butter, sliced
Optional: honey or agave nectar
   to taste
Optional: vanilla ice cream,
   caramel ice cream topping

Core each apple, leaving the base intact. Peel a one-inch strip from
around the top of each apple. Arrange apples in a slow cooker. Add
water; set aside. In a small bowl, combine brown sugar, cranberries or
raisins and spices; stir until combined. Stuff each apple with brown
sugar mixture, filling all the way to the top and pressing down to make
room for more. Top each apple with a slice of butter. Drizzle apples
with honey or agave nectar, if desired. Cover and cook on low setting
for 3 to 4 hours, or on high setting for 2 to 3 hours, until apples are
tender. Serve apples warm, topped with a scoop of ice cream and a
drizzle of caramel topping, or with some of the syrup from slow cooker.
Makes 4 to 6 servings.

Visit a nearby farmers' market
for just-harvested fruits &
vegetables, eggs, baked goods,
jams & jellies...perfect for
a farm-fresh breakfast.

Sausage Gravy & Biscuits

Jill Valentine
Jackson, TN

My hubby loves this old-time diner favorite!

1 lb. ground pork breakfast
    sausage
1/4 c. butter
1/4 c. all-purpose flour
pepper to taste

2 c. milk
10-3/4 oz. can Cheddar cheese
    soup
baked biscuits, split

Brown sausage in a skillet over medium heat. Remove sausage to paper towels and set aside; wipe out skillet. Melt butter in same skillet; stir in flour and pepper. Slowly whisk in milk and soup. Bring to a boil; cook and stir until thick and bubbly. Stir in sausage; spoon mixture into a 4-quart slow cooker. Cover and cook on low setting for 6 to 8 hours. To serve, ladle gravy over warm split biscuits. Serves 6.

Slow-Cooked Ham

Lynn Williams
Muncie, IN

Slow-cooked hams come out really moist and tender.

5-lb. fully-cooked boneless
    half ham

1 c. cola or fruit juice
Optional: 10-oz. jar ham glaze

Place ham in a slow cooker, making sure lid will close completely. Pour in cola or juice. Cover and cook on low setting for 5 to 8 hours, until ham is heated through. If desired, remove ham to a broiler pan and brush well with glaze. Place pan 10 inches below broiler. Broil for 10 to 15 minutes, watching carefully, until glaze is golden. Slice thinly and serve. Serves 8 to 10.

No peeking! Total cooking time increases by 15 to 20 minutes every time a slow cooker's lid is lifted.

Raisin-Nut Oatmeal

Joyceann Dreibelbis
Wooster, OH

What's better than waking up to a ready-to-eat hot breakfast? The oats, fruit and spices in this homey meal bake together overnight. Substitute dried cranberries for the raisins if you like.

3-1/2 c. 2% milk
3/4 c. steel-cut oats, uncooked
1 to 2 Gala, Jonagold or Yellow
    Delicious apples, peeled,
    cored and diced

3/4 c. raisins
3 T. brown sugar, packed
4-1/2 t. butter, melted
3/4 t. cinnamon
1/4 c. chopped pecans

Spray a 3-quart slow cooker with non-stick vegetable spray. Add all ingredients except pecans; stir gently. Cover and cook on low setting for 7 to 8 hours, until liquid is absorbed. Spoon oatmeal into bowls; sprinkle with pecans. Makes 6 servings.

Try using regular or low-fat milk, soy milk, almond milk or coconut milk in breakfast dishes...there's sure to be one that suits your family.

No-Sugar-Added Applesauce

Kathe Nych
Mercer, PA

This recipe is delicious and healthy! It tastes like apple pie. Use your favorite cooking apple...Rome and Yellow Transparent are great too. Cook it overnight and wake up to a delicious aroma.

30 Fuji or Northern Spy apples, peeled, cored and sliced
1/2 c. water

1-1/2 T. cinnamon, or to taste
2 t. vanilla extract
1 t. lemon juice

Combine all ingredients in a large slow cooker; mix gently. If this amount of apples is too much for your slow cooker, more apples may be added as mixture cooks down. Cover and cook on low setting for 6 to 8 hours, or 3 to 4 hours on high setting, until apples are very soft. Stir occasionally. Refrigerate in a covered container. Makes 10 to 12 servings.

Mom's Apple Butter

Lisa Ann DiNunzio
Vineland, NJ

This apple butter goes so quickly, just spread over toast, muffins, biscuits or scones and a delicious breakfast is served! You can use other apples like Fuji or Winesap in place of the Granny Smith.

14 to 16 Granny Smith apples, peeled, cored and quartered
1/2 c. dark brown sugar, packed
1/2 c. apple cider

1 T. cinnamon
1 T. lemon juice
1/8 t. ground cloves

Mix all ingredients in a large slow cooker. Cover and cook on low setting for 8 hours. Mash to desired consistency with a potato masher. Cook, uncovered, for 2 more hours. Allow to cool; store in a covered container in the refrigerator. Makes 12 servings.

For easy, no-fuss cleaning, just fill an empty slow cooker with warm, soapy water and let soak.

Rich Hot Chocolate

Kimberly Littlefield
Centre, AL

We make this hot chocolate every Christmas Eve for our family. It is a "must-have" every year.

14-oz. can sweetened
   condensed milk
7-1/2 c. milk or water
1-1/2 t. vanilla extract

1/2 c. baking cocoa
1/8 t. salt
Garnish: mini marshmallows

In a slow cooker, combine condensed milk, milk or water and vanilla. Add cocoa and salt; stir until smooth. Cover and cook on low setting for 4 hours, or on high setting for 2 hours, until very hot. Stir again. Ladle into mugs; top with marshmallows. Makes 8 to 10 servings.

A buttery slice of cinnamon toast warms you right up on a chilly morning. Spread softened butter generously on one side of toasted white bread and sprinkle with cinnamon-sugar. Broil for one to 2 minutes until hot and bubbly. Serve with mugs of hot chocolate...yummy!

HOT SANDWICHES
to Share

Auntie B's BBQ Roast Sandwiches

Bethi Hendrickson
Danville, PA

This recipe is a favorite for quick suppers or large groups. You can use a pork roast instead of beef in this recipe too...both are fantastic. Serve on hearty rolls and you have a winner!

3 to 4-lb. beef chuck roast
1 c. tomato juice
1/4 c. Worcestershire sauce
1 T. white vinegar

1 t. dry mustard
1 t. chili powder
1/4 t. garlic powder
hearty rolls, split

Spray a slow cooker with non-stick vegetable spray; add roast and set aside. In a small bowl, combine remaining ingredients except rolls. Stir until mixed well; pour mixture over roast. Cover and cook on low setting for 8 to 10 hours, or on high setting for 5 to 6 hours, until roast is very tender. Shred roast with 2 forks. Serve beef on rolls, drizzled with a little of the sauce from slow cooker. Makes 10 to 12 servings.

Slow cookers are super budget helpers! Less-expensive cuts of beef like round steak and chuck roast cook up fork-tender, juicy and flavorful...there's simply no need to purchase more expensive cuts.

Jim's Sloppy Joes

Carolyn Deckard
Bedford, IN

Knowing this is my favorite sandwich, my husband would fix these easy Sloppy Joes when we were working on different shifts.

3 lbs. ground beef
1 onion, finely chopped
1 T. garlic, minced
1-1/2 c. catsup
1/4 c. brown sugar, packed
3-1/2 T. mustard

3 T. Worcestershire sauce
1 T. chili powder
2 stalks celery, chopped
sandwich buns, split
Optional: pickles or coleslaw

In a large skillet over medium heat, brown beef with onion and garlic; drain. Meanwhile, spray a 5-quart slow cooker with non-stick vegetable spray. Add remaining ingredients except buns to slow cooker; mix well. Stir in beef mixture. Cover and cook on low setting for 6 to 7 hours. To serve, spoon beef mixture onto buns. Top with pickles or a spoonful of coleslaw, if desired. Makes 8 to 10 servings.

Keep browned ground beef on hand for easy meal prep. Just crumble several pounds of beef into a baking pan and bake at 350 degrees until browned through, stirring often. Drain well and pack recipe-size portions in freezer bags.

Pulled BBQ Chicken

Jenita Davison
La Plata, MO

Saucy and yummy on a bun! Serve with potato chips
or a tossed green salad.

6 boneless, skinless chicken
    breasts
18-oz. bottle sweet onion
    barbecue sauce, or other
    favorite sauce

1/2 c. Italian salad dressing
1/4 c. light brown sugar, packed
2 T. Worcestershire sauce
sandwich buns, split

Place chicken in a slow cooker. Combine remaining ingredients except buns; spoon over chicken. Cover and cook on low setting for 6 to 8 hours, or on high setting for 3 to 4 hours. Using 2 forks, shred chicken in the sauce; stir. Serve chicken mixture spooned onto buns. Makes 6 servings.

Enjoy hearty, comforting meals all winter long from your slow cooker...but don't put it away in the summertime! Cook up tender, mouthwatering sandwich fixin's and other summer favorites while the kitchen stays cool.

28

Hot Sandwiches
to Share

Shredded Chicken Sandwiches   *Vickie*

*Tender chicken piled high on a soft bun...just like the
sandwiches at old-fashioned church socials.*

1/4 c. olive oil
4 boneless, skinless chicken
   breasts
1 onion, chopped
10-3/4 oz. can cream of
   mushroom soup
1 c. chicken broth

1/2 c. sherry or chicken broth
2 t. soy sauce
2 t. Worcestershire sauce
salt and pepper to taste
sandwich buns, split
Optional: pickle slices, lettuce
   leaves

Heat oil in a skillet over medium-high heat. Add chicken. Cook for
5 minutes on each side, until golden. Transfer chicken to a slow
cooker; set aside. Add onion to drippings in skillet. Sauté until golden;
drain. Add soup, broth, sherry or broth, sauces and seasonings to
skillet. Stir mixture well and spoon over chicken in slow cooker. Cover
and cook on low setting for 6 to 8 hours. Shred chicken with a fork;
spoon onto buns. Garnish with pickles and lettuce, if desired. Makes
8 servings.

Whip up some homemade buttermilk dressing...wonderful on
tossed salads and a delicious dip for fresh veggies too. Blend 1/2 cup
buttermilk, 1/2 cup mayonnaise, one teaspoon dried parsley,
1/2 teaspoon onion powder, 1/4 teaspoon garlic powder,
1/8 teaspoon dill weed and a little salt and pepper.
Keep refrigerated.

Loose Meat Sandwiches

Melissa Palmer
Lake Mary, FL

*When I was growing up, my mom and dad would always
take me to a Maid-Rite restaurant where we all enjoyed these
sandwiches. To this day, my dad still enjoys these delicious burgers.*

3 lbs. lean ground beef
1/2 c. onion, chopped
1-1/2 c. water
1 cube beef bouillon
1 cube chicken bouillon
2 T. brown sugar, packed

2 T. cider vinegar
2 T. Worcestershire sauce
1 T. soy sauce
hamburger buns, split
Garnish: mustard, catsup,
  pickles

To a large slow cooker, add uncooked beef and remaining ingredients
except buns and garnish. Stir together to break up beef. Cover and
cook on high setting for 4 hours; stir occasionally. Serve beef mixture
spooned onto buns, garnished with desired toppings. Makes
12 servings.

If there's a little too much liquid inside the slow cooker and
it's almost dinnertime, tilt the lid and turn the slow cooker
to its high setting. Soon the liquid will begin to evaporate.

Hot Sandwiches
to Share

Grandma's Sloppy Joes

Jess Brunink
Whitehall, MI

When I was growing up, all the grandkids would spend the night with Grandma on Christmas Eve. We would get up and have a huge breakfast with all the family, open gifts, then have a late lunch of Sloppy Joes. I am sure Grandma tripled this recipe...we were a big family!

2 lbs. ground beef or turkey
2 c. onions, diced
2 15-oz. cans pork & beans
2 c. barbecue sauce
1/4 c. brown sugar, packed
2 t. mustard
salt to taste
sandwich buns, split

In a large skillet over medium heat, brown beef with onions; drain. Stir in remaining ingredients except buns. Spoon into a large slow cooker. Cover and cook on low setting for 4 hours. Serve mixture spooned onto buns. Makes 12 servings.

Good sound cooking makes a contented home.
– Georges-Auguste Escoffier

Simple Spiced Pulled Pork

Marie Matter
Dallas, TX

This is my go-to recipe for pulled pork. It's delicious in everything, like sandwiches, enchiladas, tacos...you name it! The roast's juices will slowly release as it cooks, so you don't even need to add any liquid to your slow cooker. So easy!

2-lb. boneless pork shoulder
    roast
2 t. canola oil

sandwich buns, split, or taco
    shells or tortillas

Pat roast dry with paper towels; set aside. Rub Spice Mix all over roast; set aside any remaining Spice Mix. Heat oil in a large skillet over medium-high heat. Brown roast on all sides for one to 2 minutes per side. Transfer roast to a slow cooker; sprinkle with remaining Spice Mix. Cover and cook on low setting for 6 to 10 hours, to desired tenderness. Remove roast to a plate; shred with 2 forks or cut into small pieces. Serve pork in buns, taco shells or tortillas, as desired. Makes 6 servings.

Spice Mix:

3 T. chili powder
1 T. smoked paprika
1 T. kosher salt
1 T. light brown sugar, packed
2 t. ground cumin

1 t. dried oregano
1 t. onion powder
1 t. garlic powder
1/2 t. cayenne pepper
1/4 t. cinnamon

Combine spices and brown sugar in a small bowl; mix well.

Bored with tacos? Serve Mexican-style sandwiches for a tasty change! Called tortas, they're hollowed-out crusty bread rolls stuffed with shredded beef or pork and cheese. Serve cold or toast like a panini sandwich...yum!

Root Beer Pulled Pork Sandwiches

Lorna Dressler
Universal City, TX

I've had this recipe for ages...everyone asks for it! Since there are only two of us, I freeze portions to be used later. For delicious pulled chicken, use four to five chicken breasts instead of the pork.

3-lb. pork butt roast, or 2 pork
   tenderloins
12-oz. bottle root beer
18-oz. bottle favorite barbecue
   sauce

hamburger buns, split and
   toasted
Garnish: coleslaw

Place roast in a slow cooker; pour root beer over it. Cover and cook on low setting for 6 to 8 hours, until easily shredded with a fork. Remove roast from cooker; discard juices. Shred roast and return to slow cooker. Pour barbecue sauce over pork. Cover and cook on low setting about 30 minutes, until heated through. Serve pork on toasted buns, topped with coleslaw. Makes 6 to 8 servings.

Pulled Pork Sandwiches

Leona Krivda
Belle Vernon, PA

I found this recipe in an old cookbook and make it often. It is simple and quick, just like I like my recipes. The family always likes it, and it's a big hit at church potlucks. Serve with coleslaw.

4-lb. pork roast
2 1-oz. pkgs. ranch salad
   dressing mix
2 1-oz. pkgs. Italian salad
   dressing mix

sandwich buns, split
Optional: barbecue sauce,
   cheese slices

Put roast in a large slow cooker; do not add anything. Cover and cook on low setting for 8 to 10 hours, until very tender. Remove roast to a plate; set aside. Add dressing mixes to cooking juices in slow cooker, along with a little water if needed. Stir very well. Pull pork apart with 2 forks. Return pork to slow cooker; mix well. Serve pork on buns, plain or garnished as desired. Serves 14 to 16.

Carol's BBQ for a Crowd

Carol Stepp
Dennison, IL

I've tweaked this recipe to suit myself and I make it often. It's a definite crowd-pleaser, tasty with thick, chunky vegetables. Great for picnics and carry-ins.

2-1/2 lbs. ground beef chuck
32-oz. bottle catsup
3/4 c. onion, chopped
3/4 c. green pepper, chopped
3/4 c. brown sugar, packed

3/4 T. chili powder
1/4 c. cider vinegar
3/4 t. Worcestershire sauce
sandwich buns, split

Lightly brown beef in a skillet over medium heat; drain well. Combine remaining ingredients except buns in a bowl; stir into beef. Spoon mixture into a slow cooker. Cover and cook on low setting for 2 to 3 hours. Serve beef mixture spooned onto buns. Makes 10 servings.

Serve up hot, tasty food at your next tailgating party...
right out of a slow cooker! Plug it into a power inverter
that draws from your car battery.

Philly Cheesesteaks

Ann Mathis
Biscoe, AR

We have made these sandwiches on a large scale and sold them at concession stands. They would sell out in an hour or less. The more thinly sliced the beef is, the less cooking time required.

1-1/2 to 2-lb. beef round steak,
   thinly sliced
1/2 t. pepper
1/2 t. garlic powder
1 onion, sliced

1 green pepper, sliced
32-oz. can beef broth
French rolls, sliced
3/4 lb. sliced Provolone or
   American cheese

Rub beef slices with pepper and garlic powder. Place in a slow cooker; add onion, green pepper and beef broth. Stir to mix. Cover and cook on low setting for 5 to 7 hours, until beef is tender. At serving time, toast rolls on a baking sheet in a 350-degree oven. To serve, lay a cheese slice on both sides of each roll. Top cheese with beef mixture, using tongs to remove beef mixture with onion and pepper onto rolls, letting juices drip back into slow cooker. Return sandwiches to oven for a few minutes, until cheese is melted. Makes 6 to 8 servings.

Mini versions of favorite hot sandwiches are fun on party platters. Look for slider buns in the bakery department, or try using small sandwich rolls.

Spicy Buffalo Chicken Sloppy Joes

DonnaMarie Ebhardt
Davenport, FL

I experimented with a buffalo chicken recipe and tweaked it to make Sloppy Joes...yum!

2 T. extra-virgin olive oil
2-1/2 lbs. ground or shredded
   chicken breast
1 c. green, red and/or yellow
   peppers, chopped
1 onion, chopped
1 T. garlic, minced
1/2 c. tomato sauce
1/4 c. chicken broth
1/4 c. thick-style hot buffalo
   wing sauce

2 T. brown sugar, packed
2 T. dry mustard
2 T. red wine vinegar
1 T. Dijon mustard
1-1/2 t. chili powder
8-oz. pkg. shredded Mexican-
   style cheese
sandwich buns, split
Garnish: lettuce leaves, sliced
   tomatoes, crumbled blue
   cheese

Heat olive oil in a large skillet over medium-high heat; stir in chicken. Cook until crumbly, golden and no longer pink. Remove chicken to a 5-quart slow cooker. Stir in remaining ingredients except buns and garnish. Cover and cook on low setting for 4 to 5 hours. During last 30 minutes, turn slow cooker to high setting; cook and stir mixture to desired thickness. Serve chicken mixture on buns, garnished with lettuce, tomato and a sprinkle of blue cheese. May omit buns; serve on lettuce-lined plates, garnished as desired. Serves 6 to 8.

A refreshing beverage for a spicy supper! Combine equal amounts of ginger ale and pineapple juice. Pour into ice-filled tumblers and garnish with fresh fruit slices stacked up on drinking straws.

Hot Ham Sandwiches

Joyceann Dreibelbis
Wooster, OH

Flavored with sweet pickle relish, these ham sandwiches are oh-so-easy to make. Great with sweet potato fries and coleslaw!

3 lbs. deli ham, thinly sliced
2 c. apple juice
2/3 c. brown sugar, packed
1/2 c. sweet pickle relish
2 t. mustard

1 t. paprika
kaiser rolls, split
Optional: additional sweet
   pickle relish

Separate ham slices and place in a 3-quart slow cooker. In a small bowl, combine apple juice, brown sugar, relish, mustard and paprika. Spoon mixture over ham. Cover and cook on low setting for 4 to 5 hours, until heated through. To serve, place 3 to 4 slices ham on each roll. Serve with additional relish, if desired. Makes 12 servings.

Turn busy-day sandwiches into a meal with sweet potato fries... deliciously different! Slice sweet potatoes into wedges, toss with olive oil and place on a baking sheet. Bake at 400 degrees for 20 to 30 minutes, until tender, turning once. Sprinkle with a little cinnamon-sugar and serve warm.

BBQ Ranch Pork Sandwiches

Cris Goode
Mooresville, IN

We love making these sandwiches in the slow cooker in the summer to avoid heating up the kitchen. They are packed with flavor and the perfect dinner meal. Leftovers are tasty too!

2-lb. pork tenderloin
seasoned salt to taste
2/3 c. balsamic vinegar catsup
    or regular catsup

1/4 c. brown sugar, packed
kaiser rolls, split
Garnish: favorite barbecue
    sauce, ranch salad dressing

Place pork in a slow cooker. Sprinkle with seasoning salt; cover with catsup and brown sugar. Cover and cook on low setting for 8 hours, or on high setting for 6 hours, until pork is very tender. Shred pork with 2 forks and stir into sauce in slow cooker. To serve, layer rolls with desired amount of barbecue sauce, pork, more barbecue sauce and salad dressing to taste. Makes 8 servings.

Crisp coleslaw is a must with barbecue! Blend a bag of shredded coleslaw mix with 1/2 cup mayonnaise, 2 tablespoons milk, one tablespoon vinegar and 1/2 teaspoon sugar. Chill for one hour before serving.

Shredded Hot Chicken Sandwiches

Jessica Kraus
Delaware, OH

This is a fantastic feed-a-crowd recipe for football weather!

3 lbs. boneless, skinless
   chicken breasts, cooked and
   shredded
1 sleeve round buttery crackers,
   crushed
2 10-3/4 oz. cans cream of
   mushroom soup

1 to 2 c. chicken broth
1/8 t. pepper
sandwich buns, split
Garnish: mustard

In a slow cooker, combine chicken, crackers, soup, one cup broth and pepper; stir gently. Cover and cook on low setting for one to 2 hours, until heated through and crackers have softened. If mixture begins to dry out, add more broth. Serve chicken mixture on hamburger buns with a dollop of mustard. Makes 12 servings.

Be a savvy shopper. Group items on your shopping list by
the area of the store where they're found...fruits and vegetables,
meat, dairy and frozen foods. You'll find it much easier
to stick to a healthy meal plan.

Italian Pull Beef

Marlys Folly
Laurium, MI

This is a great meal for a crowd! The first time I made this was for a church camp. We fed nearly 70 people by making a triple recipe and serving the beef over mashed potatoes.

5-lb. beef chuck roast
14-1/2 oz. can beef broth
1-oz. pkg. Italian salad dressing
   mix
16-oz. jar Italian giardiniera
   vegetable mix

16-oz. jar golden pepperoncini
small Italian rolls, split, buttered
   and toasted
Optional: Cheddar cheese slices

Place roast in a large slow cooker; pour in beef broth. Sprinkle dressing mix over roast; top with gardiniera and desired amount of pepperoncini. Cover and cook on low setting for 16 to 18 hours, the longer the better. Shred beef with vegetables in slow cooker. Serve beef mixture on open-faced rolls. If desired, top with au jus from slow cooker or Beef Gravy and a slice of cheese. Makes 18 to 20 servings.

Beef Gravy:

cooking juices from slow cooker
1 to 2 T. all-purpose flour

salt and pepper to taste

Strain juices from slow cooker; pour into a saucepan. Bring to a rolling boil over medium heat. Remove 1/4 cup of hot liquid to a bowl; stir in flour until mixed well. Slowly stir mixture into juices in saucepan. Cook and stir to desired thickness. Season with salt and pepper to taste.

Slow-cooker sandwiches are so deliciously juicy! To keep that juice from dripping, wrap individual servings in aluminum foil, then peel back as they're eaten.

Mom's No-Fuss Shredded Beef

Kim Smith
Greensburg, PA

So easy and so good...you'll love it!

3-lb. beef rump roast	1 T. salt
3 to 4 c. water	1 T. pepper
1 T. garlic powder	1 T. Worcestershire sauce
1 T. dry mustard	sandwich buns, split

Place roast in a slow cooker; pour in water and set aside. In a small bowl, combine seasonings and Worcestershire sauce; stir to make a paste. Rub paste on all sides of the roast. Cover and cook on low setting for 6 to 8 hours, or on high setting for 4 hours, until roast is very tender. Remove roast to a plate; shred with a fork and knife. Return shredded beef to liquid in slow cooker; stir. Serve beef mixture spooned onto buns. Makes 8 to 10 servings.

A rainy-day cure-all...toss together ingredients for a tasty slow-cooker meal, pop some popcorn and enjoy a family movie marathon. When you're ready for dinner, it's ready for you!

Kentucky BBQ Sandwiches

Michelle Hickerson
Hartford, KY

Good barbecue is a tradition here in western Kentucky. When our family made a binder with everyone's favorite recipes, I contributed my go-to barbecue recipe, liked by everyone who tries it.

3-lb. boneless pork loin
1 c. water
18-oz. bottle favorite barbecue
   sauce
1 c. brown sugar, packed

2 T. Worcestershire sauce
salt and pepper to taste
sandwich buns, split
Garnish: sliced onion, dill
   pickle slices

Place pork loin in a slow cooker; add water. Cover and cook on low setting for 8 hours. Remove pork loin from slow cooker and shred with a fork. Drain water from slow cooker; return shredded pork to slow cooker. Add remaining ingredients except buns and garnish; mix gently. Cover and cook on high setting for one hour. Serve pork mixture on buns, garnished as desired. Serves 8 to 10.

Cola BBQ Pulled Pork

Charlene McCain
Bakersfield, CA

This is the perfect dish for a picnic lunch or light supper. The cola adds a savory sweetness and tenderizes the pork roast...it almost melts in your mouth! Serve with potato chips and dill pickles.

1/2 c. onion, diced
3-lb. pork roast
1/4 t. salt
1/4 t. pepper

12-oz. can cola or root beer
1 c. favorite barbecue sauce
sandwich buns, split

Spread onion in a slow cooker. Season pork roast with salt and pepper; place on top of onion. Pour cola over roast. Cover and cook on low setting for 6 to 8 hours, until very tender. Remove roast from slow cooker; discard cooking juices and onion. Return roast to slow cooker; shred with 2 forks. Add barbecue sauce and mix well. Serve pork mixture on buns. Makes 6 to 8 servings.

Hot Sandwiches
to Share

Family-Favorite Pork Barbecue

Gladys Brehm
Quakertown, PA

A family recipe handed down by generations. I tried different ingredients until I liked the taste. The sauce is also good made with ground beef, browned and combined with the other ingredients.

2 to 3-lb. pork butt roast
1 c. celery, chopped
3/4 c. onion, chopped
1-1/2 c. catsup

1/4 c. brown sugar, packed
1/4 c. cider vinegar
1 T. mustard
hamburger buns, split

Place roast in a large slow cooker; do not add anything. Cover and cook on low setting for 6 to 8 hours, until well done. Remove roast; drain juices from slow cooker. Return roast to slow cooker; shred with 2 forks. Stir in remaining ingredients except buns. Cover and cook on low setting for an additional 4 to 6 hours, until flavors are blended and vegetables are tender. Serve pork mixture on buns. Makes 10 to 12 servings.

Many slow-cooker recipes make plenty of food for sharing.
Invite a neighbor or co-worker you've wanted to get to
know better...encourage your kids to invite a friend.
You'll be so glad you did!

43

Carolyn's Italian Beef

Tina Elyea
Greenwood, NE

This is from my mother-in-law Carolyn. She likes to tell the story about the time she had a group of ladies over for lunch and served them the "juice" from this recipe as a soup. The ladies raved about it!

4 to 6-lb. beef chuck roast,
   fat trimmed
1 T. onion, minced
2 t. garlic powder
2 t. dried oregano
2 t. dried rosemary

1 t. caraway seed
1 t. celery seed
1 t. salt
1/4 t. cayenne pepper
crusty rolls, split

Place roast in a large slow cooker; set aside. In a small bowl, combine onion and seasonings; rub mixture over roast. Add enough water to cover roast. Cover and cook on low setting for about 10 hours. Shred roast with 2 forks, discarding any fat. Serve beef mixture spooned into rolls. Serves 8 to 12.

Caramelized onions are full of flavor and easy to make. Add
1/2 cup butter, 3 pounds sliced sweet onions and one teaspoon salt
to a slow cooker. Cover and cook on low setting for 8 to
10 hours, stirring once or twice. Spoon onions over sandwiches
or stir into casseroles to add savory flavor.

French Dip Sandwiches

Kathy Grashoff
Fort Wayne, IN

After you pull apart the meat, you can add it back to the juice in the slow cooker on low setting until ready to serve. How easy! Just don't let the juice cook off, or the meat will get dry.

2 to 3-lb. beef chuck roast
2 10-1/2 oz. cans beef
   consommé

sandwich buns, split

Place roast in a greased slow cooker; pour consommé over roast. Cover and cook on low setting for 8 to 11 hours, or on high setting for 5 to 7 hours, until very tender. Remove roast to a plate; reserve juice in slow cooker. With 2 forks, pull apart roast. Serve beef mixture on buns and reserved juice as a dipping sauce. Serves 8.

Italian Beef Sandwiches

Debra Arch
Kewanee, IL

Men especially love this beef. It has lots of delicious flavor with only two ingredients! It makes your house smell wonderful as it cooks. This freezes well if you have any left.

2-lb. beef rump or sirloin
   tip roast
.6-oz. pkg. zesty Italian salad
   dressing mix

hamburger buns, split
Garnish: deli jalapeño pepper
   slices

Place roast in a slow cooker. Sprinkle dressing mix all over roast. Cover and cook on low setting for 8 to 9 hours, until roast can be pulled apart with 2 forks. Serve beef mixture on buns, topped with jalapeño slices. Makes 10 to 12 servings.

Pita halves are perfect for juicy slow-cooker sandwich fillings.

Italian Sausage, Pepper & Onion Sandwiches

Samantha Starks
Madison, WI

We love this sandwich at the state fair...but the fair only comes once a year! With this recipe, we can enjoy our favorite sandwich anytime we like.

2 lbs. Italian pork sausage links
1 green pepper, sliced
1 white onion, sliced
32-oz. jar tomato-basil
   pasta sauce
1 t. garlic powder

1 t. dried basil
1 t. dried oregano
hard rolls, split
Optional: shredded mozzarella
   cheese

Brown sausages in a large skillet over medium-high heat. Drain; add to a slow cooker. Top sausages with remaining ingredients except rolls; stir gently. Cover and cook on low setting for 4 to 5 hours. To serve, spoon sausages into rolls. Top with pepper, onion and some of the sauce. Add a sprinkle of cheese, if desired. Makes 4 to 6 servings.

Slow cookers come in so many sizes, you might want to have more than one! A 4-quart size is handy for recipes that will feed about four people, while a 5-1/2 to 6-quart one is terrific for larger families and potluck-size recipes. Just have room for one? Choose an oval slow cooker...roasts and whole chickens will fit perfectly.

Hot Sandwiches
to Share

Tammy's Chili Dogs

Tammy Epperson
Nancy, KY

*I needed a dish to take to a Christmas party for teens. This is
what I came up with...it's delicious and so simple!*

1 lb. hot dogs, cut into
   bite-size pieces
2 15-oz. cans chili sauce
15-oz. can pork & beans,
   drained

5 T. salsa con queso cheese
   sauce
hot dog buns, split

Add all ingredients except buns to a slow cooker; stir. Cover and cook
on low setting 2 hours. Serve hot dog mixture spooned into buns.
Makes 10 servings.

Steamed Hot Dogs

Erin Brock
Charleston, WV

*Great for cookouts and ballgames. We like the ones around
the edge that get browned and look grilled.*

up to 60 hot dogs
hot dog buns, split

Garnish: favorite hot dog
   toppings

Place desired number of hot dogs in a slow cooker, standing them on
end to fill the crock if necessary. Do not add any liquid. Cover and
cook on low setting for 4 hours, or on high setting for 2 hours, until
warmed through. May serve hot dogs directly from slow cooker, set to
warm. Serve in buns, garnished as desired. Makes up to 60 servings.

Hot dog buns just taste better
toasted...they won't get soggy
either. Simply butter buns lightly
and place on a hot grill for
30 seconds to one minute,
until toasted to taste.

Hot Reuben Sandwiches

Dale Duncan
Waterloo, IA

Tender slow-cooked corned beef makes the best Reubens ever!
Sometimes I'll broil the open-faced sandwiches to melt the
cheese before adding the top slice of bread.

32-oz. pkg. refrigerated
   sauerkraut
2 to 3-lb. corned beef brisket
   with spice packet
1 c. Thousand Island salad
   dressing

16 slices pumpernickel or marble
   rye bread, toasted
8 slices Swiss cheese

Place sauerkraut in a 4-quart slow cooker; top with brisket. Sprinkle spice packet over brisket. Cover and cook on low setting for 9 to 11 hours. Remove brisket to a platter; slice thinly. To serve, spread salad dressing on one side of each bread slice. With a slotted spoon, place 1/2 cup sauerkraut on 8 toast slices. Divide corned beef slices among toast slices; add cheese slices and remaining toast. Serve immediately. Makes 8 servings.

Keep the week's menus and shopping list right at
your fingertips. Criss-cross a bulletin board with wide
rick-rack and just slip lists underneath...so handy!

48

Smoky Pulled Pork

Diana Krol
Nickerson, KS

All of our family enjoys pulled pork sandwiches. Preparing them with the slow cooker just makes it that much easier! It's simple to control the fat, too, for a healthier sandwich.

1 onion, chopped
2 to 3 cloves garlic, chopped
1 t. salt
1 t. pepper
5 to 7-lb. pork butt roast
1 to 2 T. Creole seasoning or
   barbecue rub seasoning

2 T. smoke-flavored cooking
   sauce
favorite barbecue sauce to taste
sandwich buns, split

Add onion, garlic, salt and pepper to a large slow cooker. Sprinkle roast with desired seasoning; add to slow cooker. Drizzle roast with smoke-flavored sauce; add enough water to nearly fill slow cooker. Cover and cook on low setting for 8 to 10 hours, until very tender. Remove roast from slow cooker; discard liquid in slow cooker. Shred roast with 2 forks. Return shredded pork to slow cooker and stir in barbecue sauce to desired consistency. Cover and cook on low setting for about 30 minutes, until heated through. Serve pork mixture spooned into buns. Serves 8 to 12.

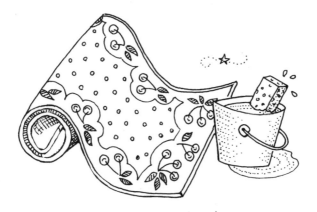

Use colorful oilcloth to dress up buffet tables...so much nicer than plastic tablecloths and it simply wipes clean.

Barbecue Beef Rolls

Jennifer Stout
Blandon, PA

This simple and very easy recipe is great for picnics.

3-lb. beef chuck roast
1 t. onion powder
1 t. garlic powder
salt and pepper to taste

18-oz. bottle favorite barbecue
  sauce
sandwich rolls, split

Place roast in a slow cooker. Sprinkle with seasonings; pour barbecue sauce over roast. Cover and cook on low setting for 6 to 8 hours, until very tender. Remove roast to a plate; shred and return to sauce mixture in slow cooker. Cover and cook on low setting for one additional hour. Serve beef mixture on rolls. Serves 10 to 12.

Napkins are a must when juicy sandwiches are on the menu!
Glue wooden alphabet letter initials to plain napkin rings
and tuck in large-size cloth napkins.

Easy Barbecued Sandwiches

Cindy Williams
Owensboro, KY

This is one of those recipes that takes only a little effort and makes for great leftovers too...if there are any! It makes the house smell really great too. Add some seasoned potato wedges and coleslaw and you have supper ready!

3 to 4-lb. pork butt roast
1/2 c. water
18-oz. bottle favorite barbecue
  sauce
1/3 c. green and/or red pepper,
  chopped

8 sandwich buns or crusty rolls,
  split and toasted
8 slices provolone cheese

Place roast in a slow cooker; add water. Cover and cook on high setting for one hour. Turn slow cooker to low setting; continue cooking for 6 to 7 hours, until roast is fork-tender. Remove roast to a plate; shred with a fork, discarding any fat. Drain liquid in slow cooker and return shredded pork to crock. Stir in barbecue sauce and pepper. Cover and cook on low setting for one more hour, or until pepper is soft. To serve, spoon pork mixture onto buns. Top with a cheese slice; let stand for a moment to allow cheese to melt. Add tops of buns. Makes 8 servings.

Fill a relish tray with crunchy fresh cut-up veggies as
a simple side dish for sandwiches. A creamy dressing can even
do double duty as a veggie dip and a sandwich spread...
try a blend of tangy Greek yogurt and basil pesto.

Open-Faced Roast Beef Sandwiches

Diana Chaney
Olathe, KS

You'll want a fork and knife for these hearty sandwiches.

3-lb. beef chuck roast
3 c. beef broth or water
.6-oz. pkg. onion soup mix
1/2 t. celery salt
1/4 c. butter, sliced

2 T. flour
salt to taste
1/4 t. pepper
6 to 8 slices frozen garlic Texas
   toast, baked

Place roast in a slow cooker. Add beef broth or water; sprinkle roast with soup mix and celery salt. Cover and cook on low setting for 6 to 8 hours, until fork-tender. Remove roast to a platter, reserving liquid in slow cooker; set aside. For gravy, melt butter in a saucepan over medium heat. Whisk in flour until smooth. Pour reserved liquid from slow cooker into saucepan, whisking well until smooth. Cook and stir over medium heat until thickened and liquid is reduced. Coarsely shred beef; stir into gravy and warm through. To serve, place each toast slice on a dinner plate; top with beef and gravy mixture. Makes 6 to 8 servings.

Mashed potatoes are the perfect partner for open-faced sandwiches. Make 'em in a jiffy! Quarter potatoes and cook in boiling water until tender, 10 to 20 minutes. Drain and mash right in the pot, then stir in butter and a little milk to desired consistency.

Roast Beef on Weck

Robin Hill
Rochester, NY

A Buffalo tradition! I was happy to find this easy slow-cooker recipe so I can make these sandwiches at home. "Weck" is short for kummelweck, rolls topped with caraway seed and coarse salt. If you can't find them, kaiser rolls will do fine.

2-1/2 lb. beef bottom round or
    rump roast
1 c. beef broth or water
1 t. onion powder
1 t. garlic powder

1/2 t. salt
1 t. pepper
1/2 c. onion, sliced
6 weck or kaiser rolls, split
Garnish: prepared horseradish

Place roast in a slow cooker; add broth or water. Combine seasonings; mix well and rub over roast. Cover and cook on low setting for 6 to 8 hours, until tender. Add onion to slow cooker; cover and cook for one more hour. Remove roast to a platter; slice thinly. To serve, top each roll generously with sliced beef; add horseradish as desired. Serve au jus from slow cooker in small bowls on the side for dipping. Makes 6 servings.

Protect a favorite cookbook from cooking spatters...
slip the opened book into a large plastic zipping bag
before you begin.

Meatball Hoagies

Virginia Watson
Scranton, PA

Hoagies, submarines, grinders, po' boys...whatever you call 'em, just call us for dinner!

1 lb. lean ground beef
1/2 c. Italian-flavored dry
   bread crumbs
1 egg, beaten
2 T. onion, minced
1 T. grated Parmesan cheese

1 t. salt
1 t. Worcestershire sauce
32-oz. jar pasta sauce
hoagie rolls, split
Garnish: sliced mozzarella
   cheese

In a large bowl, combine beef, bread crumbs, egg, onion, Parmesan cheese, salt and Worcestershire sauce. Using your hands, mix just until combined. Form into one-inch meatballs. Cook meatballs in a large skillet, turning occasionally, until browned on all sides. Remove meatballs to a slow cooker; top with pasta sauce. Cover and cook on low setting for about 2 hours, stirring after one hour. To serve, spoon several meatballs into each bun; top with a spoonful of sauce and a slice of cheese. Makes 6 to 8 servings.

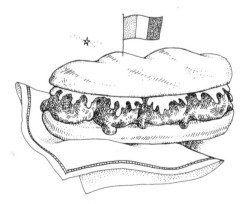

Making a big batch of meatballs? Brown them the easy way.
Simply place meatballs in a baking pan and bake at
400 degrees for 20 to 25 minutes.

Fire-Roasted Tomato & Sausage Grinders

Mel Chencharick
Julian, PA

These grinders are just the best! Made in a slow cooker, they're ready when you get home from work.

10 hot or sweet Italian pork
   sausage links
2 14-1/2 oz. cans fire-roasted
   diced tomatoes
28-oz. can crushed tomatoes
1 T. balsamic vinegar
6 cloves garlic, minced
2 t. dried basil
1 t. dried oregano

1/2 t. red pepper flakes
1/2 t. salt
1/2 t. pepper
10 slices provolone cheese,
   halved
10 French-style rolls or hoagie
   buns, split
Garnish: roasted red peppers

Place sausage links in a 6-quart slow cooker; set aside. For sauce, combine diced and crushed tomatoes with juice, vinegar, garlic and seasonings. Mix well; spoon over sausage links. Cover and cook on low setting for 6 to 8 hours, or on high setting for 3 to 4 hours. To serve, place 2 cheese slice halves and one sausage link on the bottom half of each roll. Place on a broiler pan; broil 5 inches from heat until cheese is melted, 2 to 3 minutes. Spoon some roasted peppers onto sausages; add top halves of rolls. Serve with sauce from slow cooker in small bowls for dipping. Makes 10 servings.

Keep a pair of long padded oven mitts nearby when slow cooking...they're perfect for lifting and carrying the hot crock safely.

Pork Tacos with Beans & Chiles

Donna Wilson
Maryville, TN

I love Mexican food and this one is a winner for us. This is an easy recipe to put in slow cooker and smells awesome while cooking.

4-lb. pork roast
1/2 t. onion powder
1-oz. pkg. taco seasoning mix,
   divided
16-oz. can can refried beans
4-oz. can diced green chiles

2 cloves garlic, minced
2 c. shredded Cheddar cheese
taco-size flour tortillas
Garnish: sliced avocado, salsa,
   sour cream

Place roast in a slow cooker. Sprinkle with onion powder and half of seasoning mix; set aside. Combine beans, chiles and garlic in a bowl; spread mixture over roast. Sprinkle with remaining seasoning mix. Cover and cook on low setting for 6 to 8 hours, until very tender. Remove roast to a plate; shred with 2 forks and return to slow cooker. Stir in cheese. To serve, fill tortillas with pork mixture; add desired toppings. Makes 10 to 12 servings.

Whip up a speedy black bean salad to serve with tacos. Combine one cup drained and rinsed black beans, 1/2 cup frozen corn, 1/2 cup salsa and 1/4 teaspoon cumin or chili powder. Stir well and chill until dinnertime.

HOT SANDWICHES
to Share

Savory Chicken Tacos

Gerri Roth
Flushing, MI

When working, I like to use the slow cooker so dinner will be ready when I get home. I like to make my own seasoning mix.

2 c. tomato juice
1 T. dried, minced onion
1 T. chili powder
1 t. garlic powder
1 t. onion powder
1 t. ground cumin
1/2 t. salt

4 to 6 boneless, skinless chicken
  breasts
taco-size flour tortillas
Garnish: shredded Cheddar
  cheese, chopped tomatoes,
  sour cream

Add tomato juice, onion and seasonings to a large slow cooker; stir. Add chicken; turn to coat. Cover and cook on low setting for 8 hours, or on high setting for 4 hours, until chicken is tender. Remove chicken; shred with 2 forks and return to slow cooker. Cover and cook for a few minutes, until heated through. Drain liquid from slow cooker. Spoon chicken mixture into tortillas; add desired toppings. Makes 10 to 12 servings.

Easy Chicken Tacos

Diane Cohen
Breinigsville, PA

This recipe could not be easier! The delicious seasoned chicken can also be used to make wonderful burritos, enchiladas or quesadillas.

6 boneless, skinless chicken
  breasts
16-oz. jar favorite salsa
1-oz. pkg. taco seasoning mix
flour tortillas or corn taco shells

Garnish: shredded Cheddar
  cheese, shredded lettuce,
  chopped tomatoes,
  sour cream

Place chicken in a lightly greased slow cooker. Top with salsa and seasoning mix; stir gently. Cover and cook on low setting for 6 to 8 hours. Shred chicken with 2 forks; stir into mixture in slow cooker. To serve, spoon chicken mixture into tortillas or taco shells and add desired toppings. Makes 8 to 10 servings.

Spicy Shredded Beef Tacos

Shirley Rappe
Abilene, TX

I tried some amazing tacos at a Dallas restaurant that forever changed my mind on what tacos could be. This is the recipe I came up with at home to reflect my own tastes and it's perfect for parties.

2-lb. beef flank steak
7-oz. can chipotle peppers in
   adobo sauce
1 yellow onion, chopped
1 green pepper, chopped
1 red pepper, chopped

1 jalapeño pepper, chopped
taco-size corn tortillas
Garnish: Mexican crema or sour
   cream, pico de gallo, sliced
   avocado, snipped fresh
   cilantro, shredded lettuce

Coat steak with Spice Rub; place steak in a slow cooker and set aside. Pour chipotle peppers with sauce into a blender; process until puréed. Spread chipotle purée over steak; top with chopped vegetables. Cover and cook on low setting for 8 hours, until tender. Remove steak to a cutting board; chop or shred. Return chopped beef to mixture in slow cooker; let stand several minutes so flavors can blend. Serve beef mixture on tortillas, topped with desired garnishes. Serves 6.

Spice Rub:

2 t. chili powder
1 t. ground cumin
1/4 t. onion powder

1/4 t. garlic powder
1 t. salt
1/2 t. pepper

Combine all ingredients in a cup; mix well.

Set up a taco topping bar with bowls of shredded cheese, salsa, guacamole and other garnishes. Everyone can just help themselves.

SIMMERING *Soups*

Barb's Corn Chowder

Barbara Cebula
Chicopee, MA

I make this on a fall day when I want something hot, creamy and delicious for my family. They love it! When sweet corn isn't in season, you can substitute three cups of frozen corn.

6 ears sweet corn
4 slices bacon, crisply cooked
　　and crumbled
2 potatoes, peeled and diced
1/2 c. onion, chopped
1 red pepper, chopped

2 stalks celery, diced
2 c. chicken broth
1/2 t. pepper
2 c. milk
1 T. butter, sliced

Slice corn kernels from ears, reserving cobs. Place reserved cobs, corn kernels and remaining ingredients except milk and butter in a slow cooker. Cover and cook on high setting for 7 to 8 hours, until vegetables are tender. Remove corn cobs and discard. Purée half of soup using an immersion blender or food processor. Return puréed soup to slow cooker; stir in milk and butter. Cover and continue cooking on high setting until warmed through, about 15 to 30 minutes. Makes 8 servings.

Spoon hot soup into a thermos and bring along to high school football games...a scrumptious way to warm up at half-time!

Gram's Loaded Baked Potato Soup

Sandy Coffey
Cincinnati, OH

Everyone loves baked potatoes, so this is a hearty meal in itself. Good on a frosty weekend day!

32-oz. container chicken broth
1/2 c. milk
2 T. all-purpose flour
6 potatoes, peeled and diced
1/2 c. onion, chopped

1 c. sour cream
8-oz. pkg. shredded Colby or
    mild Cheddar cheese
8 slices bacon, crisply cooked
    and crumbled

In a slow cooker, combine broth and milk. Whisk in flour; add potatoes and onion. Cover and cook for 6 to 8 hours on low setting, until potatoes are tender. Stir in sour cream. Top individual servings with cheese and bacon. Makes 4 to 6 servings.

Dried, minced onion can be a real timesaver! If the recipe has a lot of liquid, such as soups and stews, it's easy to switch. Just substitute one tablespoon of dried onion for every 1/3 cup fresh diced onion.

Creamy Chicken & Macaroni Soup

Marian Forck
Chamois, MO

A friend made this soup and let me sample it...I loved it! It is a filling soup and great with homemade bread.

2 c. cooked chicken, chopped
16-oz. pkg. frozen mixed
　vegetables
2 c. chicken broth
10-3/4 oz. can cream of chicken
　soup

3/4 c. celery, chopped
2 T. dried parsley, or to taste
2 cubes chicken bouillon
20-oz. pkg. frozen macaroni &
　cheese dinner

Combine all ingredients except macaroni & cheese dinner in a slow cooker. Cover and cook on low setting for 4 hours. Add frozen macaroni & cheese. Cover and cook for an additional 2 hours on low setting, stirring occasionally. Makes 8 servings.

Easy Vegetable Soup

Gladys Brehm
Quakertown, PA

Quick & easy...a very satisfying meal on cold days.

64-oz. can cocktail vegetable
　juice
32-oz. pkg. frozen mixed
　vegetables

2 c. cooked beef or chicken,
　chopped
1 c. curly pasta or small shell
　pasta, uncooked

Combine all ingredients in a 5-quart slow cooker. Cover and cook on high setting for 3 to 4 hours, stirring occasionally. Serves 6 to 8.

SIMMERING
Soups

Mary's Easy Chicken Chili

Brenda Hager
Nancy, KY

One of my fellow retired teachers brought this easy chili to a potluck luncheon and it was a hit. You can vary the beans and use whatever type you prefer. I like to use three different types!

2 10-oz. cans chicken breast,
  drained and flaked
4 c. chicken broth
3 15-oz. cans pinto beans,
  kidney beans, black beans,
  Great Northern beans or a
  combination, drained and
  rinsed

16-oz. jar medium salsa
Garnish: sour cream, shredded
  Cheddar cheese, chopped
  fresh chives, tortilla strips

Combine all ingredients except garnish in a slow cooker. Cover and cook on low setting for 2 hours, or until hot and bubbly. Serve garnished with desired toppings. Makes 6 to 8 servings.

When trying a new-to-you slow-cooker recipe, it's a good idea to stay nearby and check the dish often...but don't lift the lid! That way, you'll know exactly how long the recipe takes to cook in your slow cooker.

Cowboy Stew

Sue Ellen Morrison
Blue Spring, MO

*This is one of my family's favorite meals. It is wonderful with
cornbread or hushpuppies, even plain old crackers. This will fill up
a hungry family and it can simmer while you work or play.*

1 lb. ground beef
1/2 c. onion, finely chopped
salt and pepper to taste
8-oz. can tomato sauce
2 15-oz. cans ranch-style beans
    or chili beans

15-oz. can sweet corn and diced
    peppers, drained
1 baking potato, peeled and
    cubed

In a skillet over medium heat, brown beef and onion; drain. Season
beef mixture with salt and pepper; transfer to a slow cooker. Pour
tomato sauce over top. Add beans, corn, potato and just enough water
to cover ingredients. Stir gently to mix. Cover and cook on low setting
for 2 hours, or until potato is tender. Serves 4 to 6.

To make a bigger batch of a favorite slow-cooker soup or stew,
remember these handy tips for doubling or tripling the ingredients:

- Brown beef or pork to help it cook more evenly.

- Double or triple the amount of meat or poultry, but only
  increase the seasonings by half.

- Don't increase the liquid, as the slow cooker will catch all
  the juices as the dish cooks.

Chuck Wagon Chili

Jesi Allen
Clover, SC

A family favorite! We've made this chili often over the campfire, and it's just as good at home in the slow cooker. Perfect with a slice of cornbread and topped with some shredded cheese!

2 T. oil
2 lbs. stew beef cubes
1 T. salt, or to taste
1 T. pepper, or to taste
2 28-oz. cans tomato purée
24-oz. jar mild or medium
  picante sauce
2 15-oz. cans kidney beans,
  drained

2 8-oz. cans sliced mushrooms,
  drained
12-oz. bottle beer or
  non-alcoholic beer
3 T. chili powder, or to taste
2 T. ground cumin, or to taste
saltine crackers or cornbread
Optional: shredded Cheddar
  cheese, sour cream

Heat oil in a large skillet over medium-high heat. Add beef and brown on all sides; drain and season with salt and pepper. Meanwhile, in a 6-quart slow cooker, combine tomato purée, picante sauce, beans, mushrooms, beer and seasonings. Add beef to slow cooker. Cover and cook on low setting for 6 to 8 hours, until beef is very tender. Serve with crackers or cornbread, topped with shredded cheese and sour cream, if desired. Makes 6 servings.

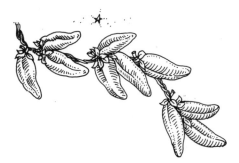

If you love super-spicy chili, give New Mexico chili powder a try. It contains pure ground red chili peppers, unlike regular chili powder which is a blend of chili, garlic and other seasonings.

Marcia's Best Vegetable Soup

Marcia Shaffer
Conneaut Lake, PA

Whenever I serve my soup to guests, they always request the recipe. We had some tree cutters working for us one summer and I served this soup to them. Several of them asked for the recipe to take home to their wives. Serve with crusty bread.

2 lbs. ground beef
1 T. oil
6 c. water
4 c. chicken or beef broth
1 c. onions, chopped
1 c. potatoes, peeled and diced
1 c. carrots, peeled and diced
1 c. celery, diced
14-1/2 oz. can whole tomatoes
15-oz. can corn, drained
15-1/4 oz. can peas, drained

14-1/2 oz. can green beans, drained
1.35-oz. pkg. onion soup mix
1 T. browning and seasoning sauce
1 T. dried basil
1 T. dried thyme
1 t. salt
1/2 t. pepper
1 bay leaf

In a skillet over medium heat, brown beef in oil; drain. Add beef and remaining ingredients to a very large slow cooker. Cover and cook on low setting for 8 hours. Discard bay leaf before serving. Makes 10 to 12 servings.

Soup is so nice when shared. Thank a friend with a basket
of warm rolls and a pot of steaming homemade soup.
What a welcome surprise on a brisk day!

Garden-Style Navy Bean Soup

Penny Sherman
Ava, MO

We love old-fashioned bean and ham soup, but this soup with spicy tomatoes and spinach is fresh tasting and different. Use plain diced tomatoes, if you prefer a milder flavor.

1 lb. dried navy beans, rinsed and sorted
6 c. water
14-1/2 oz. can diced tomatoes with spicy red pepper
2 c. cooked ham, diced
1 onion, chopped

3 stalks celery, thinly sliced
3 carrots, peeled and thinly sliced
1/2 t. dried thyme
1 t. salt
1/4 t. pepper
5-oz. pkg. baby spinach

In a large bowl, cover dried beans with water; soak for 8 hours to overnight. Drain beans, discarding water. Add beans to a slow cooker. Stir in 6 cups fresh water, tomatoes with juice and remaining ingredients except salt, pepper and spinach. Cover and cook on low setting for 9 to 10 hours, until beans are tender. Remove 2 cups of soup to a blender. Process until puréed; return to slow cooker. Add salt and pepper; gradually add spinach and stir until wilted. Makes 8 servings.

When blending hot liquids, be sure to remove the stopper from the top of your blender so steam pressure doesn't build up inside. To prevent a mess, cover the hole with a clean, folded kitchen towel before blending.

Margaret's Lentil Soup

Lory Howard
Jackson, CA

I received this hearty recipe from a great and fun friend of mine.

1/4 c. oil
3 c. cooked ham or canned
  spiced luncheon meat, diced
1/2 lb. smoked Polish or mild
  pork sausage links, sliced
  1/2-inch thick
2 onions, chopped
1 clove garlic, pressed,
  or 1 t. garlic powder
12 c. water

3/4 lb. dried lentils, rinsed and
  sorted
2 c. celery with leaves, chopped
1 to 2 tomatoes, cut into
  wedges, or 14-1/2 oz. can
  whole tomatoes
10-oz. pkg. frozen cut leaf
  spinach, partially thawed
1-1/2 t. salt
1/2 t. hot pepper sauce

Heat oil in a skillet over medium heat. Add ham or luncheon meat, sausage, onion, and garlic. Cook for 5 minutes, stirring often. Drain; add to a slow cooker. Add remaining ingredients. Cover and cook on low setting for 8 to 10 hours, until lentils are tender. This soup freezes well. Serves 6 to 8.

Slice & dice meats and veggies ahead of time and refrigerate in separate plastic zipping bags. In the morning, toss everything into the slow cooker and you're on your way.

SIMMERING
Soups

Homestyle Ham & Bean Soup

Diane Smith
Burlington, NJ

Great served with a grilled cheese and tomato sandwich!
Any leftovers freeze and reheat very well.

1 lb. dried Great Northern beans,
   rinsed and sorted
1 meaty ham bone
2 potatoes, peeled and chopped
1 carrot, peeled and chopped
2 stalks celery, chopped

1 onion, chopped
2 t. garlic, chopped
3 14-oz. cans chicken broth
5 c. water
1 t. pepper

In a large bowl, cover dried beans with water; soak for 8 hours to overnight. Drain beans, discarding water. Add beans to a slow cooker. Add remaining ingredients; stir to combine. Cover and cook on low setting for 8 hours, or on high setting for 4 hours, or until ham falls off the bone. At serving time, cut ham off the bone; discard bone. If a thicker soup is desired, use an immersion blender to slightly mash some of the beans right in the crock. Makes 8 to 10 servings.

Pick up a bunch of flowers on your next grocery shopping trip!
Even the simplest bouquet of daisies tucked into a glass
pitcher adds cheer to the dinner table.

Lightened-Up Cheeseburger Soup

Marsha Baker
Pioneer, OH

This is truly a super soup! I combined ideas from two recipes to make this one comforting dish. And I've used lighter ingredients, but only you will know that!

1 T. olive oil
1 onion, chopped
1 stalk celery, chopped
1 clove garlic, minced
1 lb. lean ground beef
3 T. all-purpose flour
3 c. fat-free chicken broth, divided
15-oz. can fire-roasted diced tomatoes, partially drained

1 c. low-fat evaporated milk
8-oz. pkg. reduced-fat pasteurized process cheese, cubed
1/2 t. paprika
Optional: 1/4 t. salt
1/4 t. pepper
Garnish: baked tortilla chips, crushed

Add oil to a Dutch oven; heat over medium-high heat for 30 seconds. Add onion, celery and garlic. Cook, stirring often, until tender, 5 to 10 minutes. Coat a 4-quart slow cooker with non-stick vegetable spray; spoon in onion mixture and set aside. In the same skillet, brown beef over medium-high heat, breaking up beef as it cooks. Drain and add beef to slow cooker. In a small cup, combine flour and 1/2 cup broth; stir until smooth and lump-free. Pour flour mixture into same skillet; add remaining broth. Bring to a simmer, scraping up any browned bits in bottom of skillet; pour into slow cooker. Stir in remaining ingredients except tortilla chips. Cover and cook on low setting for 2 hours. Serve soup topped with crushed chips. Serves 8.

A properly working slow cooker uses about as much electricity as a light bulb, making it more economical... and cooler...than using the stove!

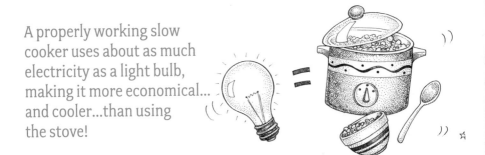

70

Stuffed Cabbage Soup

Deborah Douma
Pensacola, FL

I don't recall where I got this recipe...my copy is scribbled out on a piece of lined paper. It is hearty and delicious.

5 c. boiling water
4 cubes beef bouillon
1/2 head cabbage, chopped
1-1/2 lbs. ground turkey
28-oz. can crushed tomatoes
1/2 c. quick-cooking barley,
    cooked

1 onion, chopped
2 cloves garlic, minced
2 t. sugar
1 t. pepper
1/4 t. hot pepper sauce

Combine boiling water and bouillon cubes in a large bowl; set aside. Place cabbage in a slow cooker; set aside. Brown turkey in a large skillet over medium heat. Stir in bouillon mixture along with undrained tomatoes and remaining ingredients. Mix well and spoon over cabbage in slow cooker. Cover and cook on low setting for 8 to 9 hours. Stir before serving. Makes 8 servings.

Not sure if your slow cooker is heating to the right temperature? Add 8 cups of water to it, cover and heat on low setting for 8 hours. Immediately check the water temperature with an instant-read kitchen thermometer. It should read 185 degrees if the slow cooker is heating properly.

Harvest Pork & Squash Stew

JoAnn

*Try this flavorful stew on a fall day after the first snap of cold air.
I like to serve it with warm sweet potato biscuits.*

1-1/2 lbs. pork shoulder roast,
   cubed
salt and pepper to taste
1 T. olive oil
1 onion, chopped
1-1/2 c. butternut squash,
   peeled and cubed
16-oz. pkg. baby carrots

8 new redskin potatoes,
   quartered
12-oz. jar homestyle pork gravy
1/4 c. water
1/4 c. catsup
1 t. dried sage
1/2 t. dried thyme

Season pork with salt and pepper. Heat oil in a large skillet over medium heat; add pork and onion. Cook, stirring often, until pork is browned on all sides, about 5 minutes; drain. Combine pork mixture with remaining ingredients in a large slow cooker; stir gently. Cover and cook on low setting for 7 to 8 hours. Makes 6 to 8 servings.

Crusty bread is a must-have alongside hearty soups.
Heat an oven-safe stoneware bowl and tuck slices inside
to keep them toasty at the table.

Winter Vegetable Stew

*Linda Belon
Winterville, OH*

*A scrumptious chunky meatless stew...perfect for snow-day
lunches and chilly tailgating parties.*

28-oz. can Italian peeled whole
   tomatoes, drained and liquid
   reserved
14-1/2 oz. can vegetable or
   chicken broth
4 redskin potatoes, cut into
   1/2-inch cubes
2 c. celery, cut into 1/2-inch
   pieces
1-1/2 c. carrots, peeled and cut
   into 1/2-inch pieces

1 c. parsnips, peeled and cut
   into 1/2-inch pieces
2 leeks, cut into 1/2-inch pieces
1/2 t. salt
1/2 t. dried thyme
1/2 t. dried rosemary
3 T. cornstarch
3 T. cold water

Coarsely chop tomatoes and add to a 5-quart slow cooker along with
reserved liquid. Add remaining ingredients except cornstarch and cold
water. Cover and cook on low setting for 8 to 10 hours. About
30 minutes before serving, dissolve cornstarch in cold water; gradually
stir into stew until well blended. Cover and cook on high setting about
20 minutes, stirring occasionally, until thickened. Makes 8 servings.

Leeks are delicious in recipes, but may be sandy when purchased.
To quickly clean leeks, slice them into 2-inch lengths and soak in
a bowl of cold water. Swish them in the water and drain. Refill the
bowl and swish again until the water is clear. Drain and
pat dry...they're recipe-ready!

Uncle Jim's Taco Soup

Beverley Williams
San Antonio, TX

This was my Great-Uncle Jim's recipe. Cooking it brings back fond memories of him. Garnish with crushed tortilla chips.

2 lbs. ground beef
15-1/2 oz. can hominy
15-1/4 oz. can corn
15-oz. can ranch-style beans
14-1/2 oz. can diced tomatoes
   with green chiles

1/2 c. onion, chopped
1 c. water
1-oz. pkg. ranch salad dressing
   mix
1-oz. pkg. taco seasoning mix

Brown beef in a skillet over medium heat. Drain well; add to a slow cooker. Add all canned vegetables; do not drain. Stir in remaining ingredients. Cover and cook on high setting for 3 to 4 hours, stirring occasionally. Serves 6.

Need to feed a few extra guests? It's easy to stretch a slow cooker full of soup! Some quick add-ins are canned beans, instant rice, ramen noodles or orzo pasta. Add cooked ingredients to slow cooker and simmer for just a few minutes until heated through.

Soups

Chicken Enchilada Chili

Panda Spurgin
Berryville, AR

I always use bone-in chicken thighs or legs...I find the flavor is so much better. Serve with cornbread or corn chips.

2 15-oz. cans pinto beans,
   black beans, chili beans
   or a combination
2 14-1/2 oz. cans diced
   tomatoes
2 10-oz. cans enchilada sauce
1 c. celery, diced
1 onion, diced

1 to 2 T. chili powder
1 t. ground cumin
4 chicken thighs and/or legs,
   skin removed
Garnish: sour cream, shredded
   Cheddar cheese, diced
   avocado, chopped fresh
   cilantro

In a slow cooker, combine undrained beans, undrained tomatoes, enchilada sauce, vegetables and seasonings. Stir gently; place chicken pieces on top. Cover and cook on low setting for 8 hours. Remove chicken to a plate and shred, discarding bones. Return chicken to slow cooker; stir. Serve garnished with desired toppings. Makes 10 servings.

Swap party specialties with a friend! For example, offer to trade a crock of your super-secret-recipe chili for your best girlfriend's very best cheese dip. It's a super way to save party-planning time and money.

French Lentil Soup

Marcia Shaffer
Conneaut Lake, PA

My great-great-grandmother was from France. This is a very old recipe passed down through many generations.

6 T. oil
1 onion, chopped
2 cloves garlic, minced
12 c. water
1-1/2 c. dried lentils, rinsed
   and sorted
1 potato, peeled and diced
1 stalk celery, finely chopped
1 turnip, peeled and diced

1 carrot, peeled and finely
   chopped
1 c. tomato sauce
salt and pepper to taste
1 bay leaf
1 bunch fresh sorrel or spinach,
   torn
1/2 c. cooked rice

Heat oil in a skillet over medium heat. Add onion and cook until soft, about 5 minutes. Add garlic; cook 3 minutes. Add onion mixture and remaining ingredients except sorrel or spinach and rice to a slow cooker. Cover and cook on low setting for 8 hours. Discard bay leaf. Shortly before serving time, add sorrel or spinach and cooked rice to slow cooker. Cover and cook for several minutes, until greens wilt; stir well. Makes 6 to 8 servings.

Frozen leftovers from a slow-cooked meal make great quick lunches and dinners. Thaw and reheat them using the microwave, stovetop or oven...slow cookers don't work well for reheating frozen foods.

SIMMERING
Soups

Jess's Vegan Pea Soup

Jess Brunink
Whitehall, MI

My version of pea soup...I love this stuff! It's cheap, filling and will feed a large family. I have four kiddos and a husband and we all love it! When we have leftovers, I even eat it for breakfast. If you are not vegan, a little diced turkey ham is also really tasty.

2 lbs. dried split peas, rinsed
    and sorted
8 c. water
3 cloves garlic, minced

3 potatoes, peeled and diced
1 onion, diced
salt to taste

Combine all ingredients in a slow cooker; stir gently. Cover and cook on low setting for 8 hours, or until peas are tender. Makes 8 servings.

Creamy Tomato-Tortellini Soup

Lori Haines
Johnson City, TN

We make this soup often at work. Start it at 8 a.m. and it is ready by lunchtime at noon. It's wonderful on those cold, snowy days.

32-oz. container chicken broth
18-oz. pkg. refrigerated cheese
    tortellini, uncooked
28-oz. can petite diced tomatoes

2 10-3/4 oz. cans tomato soup
2 8-oz. containers chive and
    onion cream cheese spread,
    softened

Combine broth, tortellini and tomatoes with juice in a slow cooker. Cover and cook on high setting for about 3 hours, until tortellini starts swelling. Stir in soup; add cream cheese by spoonfuls. Cover and cook on high setting one more hour. Stir until cream cheese is smooth before serving. Makes 6 to 8 servings.

Turkey Noodle Soup

Erin Kelly
Jefferson City, MO

My mom and I first made this recipe for dinner after going to a fall festival. It was a warm and delicious end to a great day with her, and a good way to use up leftover turkey!

5 c. chicken broth
10-3/4 oz. can cream of
chicken soup
15-oz. can corn, drained
salt and pepper to taste
1/2 c. onion, finely chopped
1/2 c. green onions, sliced

1/2 c. carrot, peeled and finely
chopped
1/2 c. celery, finely chopped
1-1/2 c. medium egg noodles,
uncooked
2 c. cooked turkey, chopped

In a slow cooker, combine all ingredients except noodles and turkey. Cover and cook on low setting for 4 to 5 hours. Stir in noodles and turkey. Turn slow cooker to high setting; cover and cook for one additional hour. Makes 6 servings.

Good manners: The noise you don't make
when you're eating soup.
— Bennett Cerf

Zippy Sausage & Vegetable Soup

Roberta Simpkins
Mentor on the Lake, OH

I add twice as much horseradish when making this hearty soup for my husband and son. They like an extra kick! Serve with crackers.

14-1/2 oz. can diced tomatoes
10-3/4 oz. can cream of
  mushroom soup
1/2 lb. smoked turkey sausage,
  cut into 1/2-inch slices
15-oz. can black beans, drained
  and rinsed

2 c. potatoes, peeled and diced
1 c. onion, chopped
1 c. red pepper, chopped
1/2 c. water
2 t. prepared horseradish
2 t. honey
1 t. dried basil

Combine all ingredients in a slow cooker; mix well. Cover and cook on low setting for 7 to 8 hours, until potatoes are tender. Makes 6 to 8 servings.

Serve steaming soup in hollowed-out rounds of sourdough bread. To make yummy croutons, cut the scooped-out bread into one-inch cubes. Season to your liking; lightly toast in an oiled, hot skillet.

Vegetarian Quinoa Chili

Marie Matter
Dallas, TX

These hearty chili couldn't be easier. Just combine everything in your slow cooker, and hours later you'll have a healthy, tasty meal that everyone in your family will love. Enjoy!

2 14-1/2 oz. cans diced
    tomatoes with green chiles
15-oz. can tomato sauce
15-oz. can kidney beans,
    drained and rinsed
15-oz. can black beans, drained
    and rinsed
1-1/2 c. vegetable broth
1 c. frozen corn
1 c. quinoa, uncooked and
    rinsed
1 onion, diced
3 cloves garlic, minced

2 T. chili powder
2 t. ground cumin
1-1/2 t. smoked paprika
1-1/2 t. sugar
1/4 t. cayenne pepper
1/2 t. ground coriander
1/2 t. kosher salt
1/4 t. pepper
Garnish: shredded Cheddar
    cheese, sour cream, sliced
    avocado, chopped fresh
    cilantro

Combine undrained tomatoes and remaining ingredients except garnish in a slow cooker; stir together. Cover and cook on low setting for 6 to 8 hours, or on high setting for 3 to 4 hours. To serve, ladle into soup bowls; garnish as desired. Makes 6 servings.

It's simple to make your favorite stovetop soup in a slow cooker. Most soups that simmer for one to 2 hours will be done in 8 to 10 hours on low, or 4 to 5 hours on high. Wait until the last 30 minutes to add dairy ingredients like sour cream and tender veggies like peas.

Cheesy Broccoli Soup

Karen Sampson
Waymart, PA

This rich, creamy soup is a sure crowd-pleaser.

1/4 c. butter, sliced
1 c. onion, finely chopped
2/3 c. all-purpose flour
3 10-1/2 oz. cans chicken broth
16-oz. pkg. frozen chopped
    broccoli, rinsed with hot
    tap water

1-1/4 c. celery, finely chopped
16-oz. pkg. pasteurized process
    cheese, cubed
2 c. whipping cream

Melt butter in a small skillet over medium heat. Add onion; cover
and cook until glossy. Transfer onion and butter to a slow cooker.
Gradually add flour to slow cooker, whisking constantly. Add broth
and stir until smooth. Add broccoli and celery; stir to combine. Cover
and cook on low setting for 6 to 7 hours. Add cheese cubes and stir
until melted; stir in cream. Cover and continue cooking for another
30 minutes. Makes 6 servings.

If you enjoy creamy soups, try substituting canned evaporated
milk for whipping cream, half-and-half or whole milk. It holds up
well in slow-cooker recipes, doesn't need refrigeration
and is lower in fat too.

Cider Pork Stew

Mel Chencharick
Julian, PA

This recipe gives the familiar taste of stew a new twist.
Try it...it's very good!

2 to 2-1/2 lbs. pork shoulder
   roast, cubed and fat trimmed
Optional: 1 T. oil
3 potatoes, peeled and cut into
   1/2-inch cubes
3 carrots, peeled and cut into
   1/2-inch slices
2 onions, sliced
1/2 c. celery, coarsely chopped

2/3 c. apple, peeled, cored and
   coarsely chopped
2 c. apple cider or apple juice
3 T. quick-cooking tapioca,
   uncooked
1 t. caraway seed
1 t. salt
1/4 t. pepper
Optional: snipped fresh chives

If desired, brown pork in oil in a large skillet over medium heat. Place pork in a 5-quart slow cooker. Add vegetables and apple; set aside. In a bowl, combine remaining ingredients except optional chives. Pour over pork mixture in slow cooker. Cover and cook on low setting for 10 to 12 hours, or on high setting for 5 to 6 hours, until pork is tender. If desired, top each serving with a sprinkle of snipped chives. Makes 6 to 8 servings.

Need to add a little flavor boost to a soup or stew? Just add a splash of Worcestershire sauce, lemon juice or balsamic vinegar.

SIMMERING
Soups

Weeknight Beef Stew

Karen Wilson
Defiance, OH

A hearty recipe that's easy to toss together.

2 lbs. stew beef cubes
14-1/2 oz. can beef broth
11-1/2 oz. can vegetable
   cocktail juice
3 to 4 potatoes, peeled and
   cubed
2 stalks celery, chopped
2 carrots, peeled and chopped
1 sweet onion, chopped

3 bay leaves
1/2 t. dried thyme
1/2 t. chili powder
1 t. salt
1/4 t. pepper
2 T. cornstarch
1 T. cold water
1/2 c. frozen peas
1/2 c. frozen corn

In a large slow cooker, combine all ingredients except cornstarch, cold water, peas and corn. Cover and cook on low setting for 7 to 8 hours, until beef is tender. Discard bay leaves. In a small bowl, stir together cornstarch and cold water until smooth. Stir mixture into stew; add corn and peas. Cook on high setting for 30 minutes, or until thickened. Makes 4 to 6 servings.

Browning isn't required for slow-cooker stew cubes, but it does add lots of flavor. For best results, pat stew cubes dry with a paper towel before browning. Don't crowd the pieces in the pan, and be sure to stir up all the tasty browned bits at the bottom.

Mom's Oxtail Soup

Bobbie Keefer
Byers, CO

*Soups were an important part of my German mom's recipe collection.
Cabbage was often used in her delicious soups. Oxtail Soup, or
Ochsenschwanzsuppe, is a favorite family heirloom recipe.*

2 lbs. beef oxtails
salt and pepper to taste
1 T. butter
1 T. oil
1 onion, chopped
2 cloves garlic, minced
14-1/2 oz. can beef broth

2 14-1/2 oz. cans diced
   tomatoes
1 head cabbage, chopped
3 carrots, peeled and diced
2 t. dried parsley
1 t. dried thyme
1 t. bay leaves, crumbled

Season oxtails with salt and pepper; set aside. Heat butter and oil in a
large skillet over medium-high heat. Brown oxtails on all sides; remove
to a slow cooker, reserving drippings in skillet. Add onion and garlic
to reserved drippings. Cook for 5 to 10 minutes, stirring often, until
caramelized. Add broth to skillet; simmer for a few minutes, stirring
up any browned bits in bottom of skillet. Add skillet mixture to slow
cooker along with undrained tomatoes and remaining ingredients.
Cover and cook on high heat for 8 hours, or until vegetables are tender
and meat pulls easily away from the bones. Discard bones before
serving. Makes 8 servings.

A collection of coffee mugs is fun for serving soup! Pick up
one-of-a-kind novelty or souvenir mugs for a song at yard sales.

84

SIMMERING

Soups

Bean & Ham Soup

Pat Furmanski
Haddon Heights, NJ

I have made this soup for years whenever I had a holiday ham bone available.

1 lb. dried navy or Great
   Northern beans, rinsed
   and sorted
1 yellow onion, diced
2 cloves garlic, minced
1 T. canola or olive oil
14-1/2 oz. can diced tomatoes

1 ham bone
2 c. cooked ham, diced
1/2 to 1 t. dried thyme
pepper to taste
2 T. wine vinegar or cider
   vinegar

In a large bowl, cover dried beans with water; soak for 8 hours to overnight. Drain beans, discarding water; add to a slow cooker and set aside. In a skillet over medium heat, sauté onion and garlic in oil until onion is transparent. Add onion mixture to a 6-quart slow cooker along with tomatoes with juice, ham bone, ham, thyme and pepper. Stir gently; add enough cold water to cover ingredients. Cover and cook on low setting for 9 to 10 hours. Just before serving, discard ham bone; stir in vinegar. Makes 10 servings.

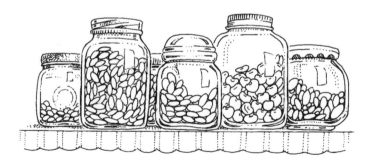

Instead of soaking, dried beans can be slow-cooked overnight on low. Cover with water and add a teaspoon of baking soda. In the morning, just drain and proceed with the recipe.

Polish Sausage & Cabbage Soup

Marcia Shaffer
Conneaut Lake, PA

A hand-me-down recipe from Poland.

1-1/4 to 1-1/2 lbs. smoked
    Polish pork sausage links,
    halved lengthwise and sliced
    1/2-inch thick
4 c. fat-free chicken broth
4 c. cabbage, chopped

2 c. potatoes, peeled and cubed
1 to 2 onions, chopped
1 carrot, peeled and shredded
2 T. caraway seed, crushed
salt and pepper to taste

Combine all ingredients in a slow cooker. Cover and cook on low setting for 7 to 8 hours. Makes 6 to 8 servings.

Prefer not to leave the slow cooker on while you're away? Simple...put it to work overnight! In the morning, refrigerate food in a fridge container...reheat at suppertime.

Hearty Tomato-Beef Stew

Bethi Hendrickson
Danville, PA

*This stew is fantastic on a cold winter's evening. Serve with
fresh-baked bread or drop biscuits...your family will be all smiles.*

1 lb. stew beef cubes
Optional: 1 T. oil
6 to 7 potatoes, peeled and diced
5 to 6 carrots, peeled and diced

2 to 3 stalks celery, diced
2 10-3/4 oz. cans tomato soup
1 T. celery seed

Spray a slow cooker with non-stick vegetable spray; set aside. If
desired, brown beef in oil in a skillet over medium heat. Combine beef,
potatoes, carrots and celery in a slow cooker; mix well. Add soup and
celery seed; mix well again. Cover and cook on low setting for 7 to
8 hours. Makes 8 to 10 servings.

Warm homebaked biscuits are a down-home delight with stew.
They're easy to make with biscuit baking mix. Here's a secret...
for the flakiest biscuits, don't overwork the dough. Simply
stir to mix and roll or pat out gently.

Easy 2 x 4 Soup

Melinda Schadler
Fargo, ND

*A nice change of pace from ordinary soups! This is a spicy soup,
so if your family prefers a milder taste, replace one can of the
tomatoes with a can of plain petite diced tomatoes.*

1 to 2 lbs. ground beef
1/2 c. onion, chopped
salt and pepper to taste
10-oz. can diced tomatoes with
   green chiles
10-oz. can diced tomatoes with
   green chiles and cilantro
2 19-oz. cans minestrone soup

2 15-oz. cans ranch-style beans
   or pinto beans
1-oz. pkg. ranch salad dressing
   mix
Garnish: shredded Cheddar
   cheese, light sour cream,
   crushed tortilla chips

In a large skillet over medium heat, brown beef with onion. Drain;
season with salt and pepper. Add tomatoes with juice and remaining
ingredients except garnish; simmer for about 10 minutes. Transfer
mixture to a large slow cooker. Cover and cook on low setting for 2 to
3 hours, until heated through. Garnish individual servings with desired
toppings. Makes 6 to 8 servings.

Invite friends to a fireside soup supper on a chilly evening!
Place comfy cushions on the floor to sit on and bring
the crock of soup right into the family room.

SIMMERING
Soups

Spicy Chicken & Green Chile Soup

Darcy Geiger
Columbia City, IN

I use the slow cooker all week long, as we have three children going in three different directions. I often come up with my own recipes to create some variety. This soup is very tasty!

3 c. cooked chicken, diced or shredded
2 15-oz. cans whole tomatoes
2 15-oz. cans ranch-style beans
32-oz. container chicken broth
16-oz. jar green salsa
4-oz. can diced green chiles
2 15-oz. cans garbanzo beans, drained
Garnish: crumbled queso fresco cheese or shredded white Cheddar cheese, sour cream, crushed tortilla chips

In a large slow cooker, combine chicken, tomatoes with juice and remaining ingredients except garnish. Cover and cook on low setting for 6 to 8 hours. Stir. Garnish with cheese, a dollop of sour cream and some crushed tortilla chips. Makes 4 to 6 servings.

Lots of great recipes start with cooked and cubed chicken. Save time and money...buy chicken in bulk and simmer it all at once. When cooled, pack recipe-size portions of chicken in freezer bags and freeze. They'll thaw quickly when you're ready to use them.

Creamy Chicken Chili

Chris Cleveland
Wilton, ND

This out-of-the-ordinary chili is always a hit at potlucks!

2 boneless, skinless chicken
   breasts
11-oz. can corn
10-oz. can diced tomatoes
   with green chiles
1 c. canned black beans, drained
   and rinsed
1-oz. pkg. ranch salad
   dressing mix

1 t. chili powder
1 t. onion powder
1 t. ground cumin
8-oz. pkg. cream cheese,
   softened and cubed
Garnish: tortilla chips

Place chicken in a slow cooker; set aside. In a bowl, combine undrained corn, undrained tomatoes and beans. Top with dressing mix and seasonings; stir together and pour over chicken. Place cream cheese on top. Cover and cook on low setting for 6 to 8 hours. Stir in cream cheese. Shred chicken with 2 forks; stir into chili. Serve with tortilla chips. Makes 4 to 6 servings.

Keep a picnic basket packed with a blanket, tableware and other picnic supplies. You'll be ready for a family picnic at a moment's notice...just grab dinner in the slow cooker and go!

Simmering
Soups

Mom's So-Simple Chili

Nicole Wood
Ontario, Canada

My mother taught me this super-easy recipe. It's a great warm-up on cold days and even better when served with warm buttered rolls.

1 lb. extra-lean ground beef
1 onion, diced
salt and pepper to taste
28-oz. can crushed tomatoes
19-oz. can kidney beans

1-1/4 oz. pkg. chili seasoning
  mix
Garnish: shredded Cheddar
  cheese

In a skillet over medium heat, brown beef with onion. Drain; season with salt and pepper. Add beef mixture to a slow cooker along with undrained tomatoes, undrained beans and seasoning mix. Stir well. Cover and cook on low setting for 2 to 3 hours, until heated through. Garnish individual servings with cheese. Makes 4 to 6 servings.

Serve taco salads in a new way. Layer chili, lettuce and diced tomatoes in large clear plastic cups. Top with shredded cheese, chopped avocado and a dollop of sour cream. Provide sturdy plastic forks...guests can stroll and eat!

Buffalo Chicken Stew

Lori Haines
Johnson City, TN

This is really good to make and then freeze in quart bags...just microwave a bag for a quick supper. Don't add the blue cheese until serving. Yummy on a cold night when you don't want to cook.

2 to 3 lbs. boneless chicken
    tenders
1/2 c. butter, divided
1-1/2 c. celery, chopped and
    divided
1-1/2 c. onion, chopped and
    divided
2 t. salt
1 t. pepper
1 c. carrots, peeled and chopped
2 t. garlic powder
4 15-oz. cans navy or Great
    Northern beans

2 14-1/2 oz. cans petite diced
    tomatoes
5-oz. bottle buffalo-style
    hot pepper sauce
1 T. chili powder
1 T. ground cumin
8-oz. bottle blue cheese salad
    dressing
4-oz. container blue cheese
    crumbles

In a slow cooker, combine chicken, 1/4 cup butter, 1/2 cup celery, 1/2 cup onion, salt and pepper. Add enough water to cover ingredients. Cover and cook on low setting for 7 hours to overnight, until chicken is tender. Remove chicken to a plate, reserving mixture in slow cooker. Shred chicken and return to slow cooker; set aside. Melt remaining butter in a skillet over medium heat. Add carrots and remaining celery and onion; season with garlic powder. Sauté until vegetables are tender, about 5 minutes. Add sautéed vegetables to slow cooker along with undrained beans and tomatoes, hot sauce and spices. Stir; add enough water to generously cover ingredients. Cover and cook on low setting for 6 to 8 hours, or on high setting for 3 to 4 hours. Shortly before serving time, combine salad dressing and blue cheese in a bowl. Serve bowls of stew topped with a dollop of dressing mixture. Serves 10.

Keep a big stack of bandannas on hand
to use as napkins when serving chili
and other western-style foods.

SIMMERING
Soups

Brunswick Stew

Lacey Houseman
Thomaston, GA

I love to make this hearty chicken stew on a chilly day.
It's so easy to make...warms the soul too!

1 onion, chopped
3 boneless, skinless chicken
   breasts
2 14-1/2 oz. cans crushed
   tomatoes
14-3/4 oz. can creamed corn
14-oz. can chicken broth
12-oz. bottle chili sauce

1/4 c. Worcestershire sauce
1/4 c. margarine, sliced
1 T. vinegar
2 t. dry mustard
1/2 t. salt
1/2 t. pepper
1/2 t. hot pepper sauce

Spread onion in the bottom of a slow cooker; arrange chicken on top.
Add tomatoes with juice and remaining ingredients; stir gently. Cover
and cook on high setting for 4 hours, or until chicken is tender.
Remove chicken to a plate and shred with 2 forks; stir back into
mixture in slow cooker. Makes 10 to 12 servings.

Fluffy dumplings are tasty in any hearty soup. About 30 minutes
before soup is done, mix up 2 cups biscuit baking mix with
3/4 cup milk. Drop by tablespoonfuls onto simmering soup.
Cover and cook on high setting for 20 to 25 minutes...done!

Pasta Fagioli Soup

Marla Kinnersley
Littleton, CO

This is one of my favorite go-to soups! I make it a lot for Sunday dinners and then we have leftovers for busy Mondays. It is very satisfying served with bread sticks and a crisp tossed salad.

1 lb. ground beef
1 yellow onion, chopped
14-1/2 oz. can diced tomatoes
26-oz. jar spaghetti sauce
2 14-1/2 oz. cans beef broth
15-1/2 oz. can kidney beans,
   drained and rinsed
1 c. carrots, peeled and grated
1 c. celery, sliced

1 T. white balsamic vinegar
1 t. dried basil
1 t. dried oregano
1/2 t. dried thyme
1/2 t. pepper
1/2 t. hot pepper sauce
1-1/2 c. small shell pasta,
   uncooked
2 t. fresh parsley, chopped

In a skillet over medium heat, brown beef with onion. Drain; add beef mixture to a 5-quart slow cooker. Add tomatoes with juice and remaining ingredients except pasta and parsley; stir. Cover and cook on low setting for 7 to 8 hours. About 15 minutes before serving, stir in pasta and parsley. Cover and cook on low setting for 15 minutes more, or until pasta is tender. Makes 8 servings.

Crunchy bread sticks are tasty soup dippers! Stand them up in a tall, wide flower vase...they'll take up little space on a soup buffet.

EASY WEEKNIGHT

Meals

Courtney's Chicken & Noodles

Leona Krivda
Belle Vernon, PA

My granddaughter Courtney got this recipe out and thought she'd like it. It took many tries for me to get it right for her, but she said this was it, she really likes it a lot and the rest of us do too.

8 to 9 boneless, skinless chicken
   breasts
garlic powder, salt and pepper
   to taste
2 14-1/2 oz. cans chicken broth
2 10-3/4 oz. cans cream of
   chicken soup

8-oz. pkg. cream cheese,
   softened and diced
1/2 c. butter, diced
24-oz. pkg. kluski egg noodles,
   uncooked
Optional: additional chicken
   broth

Season chicken breasts lightly with garlic powder, salt and pepper. Arrange chicken in a large slow cooker sprayed with non-stick vegetable spray. Add broth, soup, cream cheese and butter; stir. Cover and cook on high setting for 3 to 4 hours, until chicken is very tender. Remove chicken to a large plate; shred with 2 forks and return to mixture in slow cooker. Season with additional garlic powder and a little pepper; stir in uncooked noodles. Turn slow cooker to low setting. Cover and cook another one to 2 hours, just until noodles are soft. If mixture is too thick, add a little more broth. Makes 6 to 8 servings.

Slow cookers are ideal for any country supper potluck.
Tote them filled with your favorite hearty stew, pulled pork,
spiced cider or cobbler...scrumptious!

EASY WEEKNIGHT
Meals

Herbed Chicken & Wild Rice

Shirley Howie
Foxboro, MA

This savory recipe is quick & easy to prepare and it has become one of my favorites for the slow cooker.

6-oz. pkg. long grain and
   wild rice mix
6 boneless, skinless chicken
   breasts
1 T. oil
1 t. butter
1/2 lb. sliced mushrooms
10-3/4 oz. can cream of
   chicken soup

1-1/4 c. water
3 slices bacon, crisply cooked
   and crumbled, or
   3 T. bacon bits
1 t. dried parsley
1/2 t. dried thyme
1/2 t. dried basil

Place uncooked rice in a 5-quart slow cooker; set aside seasoning packet. In a large skillet over medium heat, brown chicken breasts in oil and butter on both sides. Add chicken to slow cooker. In the same skillet, sauté mushrooms until tender; spoon over chicken. In a small bowl, whisk together soup, water, bacon, herbs and contents of seasoning packet. Pour over mushrooms. Cover and cook on low setting for 4 hours, or until chicken juices run clear when pierced. Makes 6 servings.

Try this easy substitution for canned cream soups. In a bowl, combine one tablespoon softened butter, 3 tablespoons flour, 1/2 cup low-fat milk, 1/2 cup chicken broth and salt and pepper to taste. Blend well and use as you would one 10-3/4 ounce can of cream soup.

Healthy Crock Burritos

Barbara Hightower
Broomfield, CO

My daughter Gigi gave me this easy recipe for chicken burritos after she served them to us for family dinner at her house. Great for filling up the slow cooker and coming home to a hot meal...they're low-calorie and really delicious!

4 boneless, skinless chicken
  breasts
15-oz. can black beans, drained
  and rinsed
7-oz. can red enchilada sauce

7-oz. can green enchilada sauce
burrito-size flour tortillas
Garnish: chopped onions,
  shredded lettuce, sour cream,
  shredded Cheddar cheese

Arrange chicken breasts in a slow cooker. Layer beans and sauces over chicken. Cover and cook on low setting for 6 to 8 hours. Remove chicken to a plate; shred with a fork. Return chicken to slow cooker and stir to mix. To serve, spoon chicken mixture into tortillas; add desired toppings and roll up. Makes 4 to 6 servings.

A basket of warmed flour tortillas is a must-have with burritos and fajitas. Simply wrap tortillas in aluminum foil and pop into a 250-degree oven for about 15 minutes...easy!

Mexican Dump Chicken

Mindy Humphrey
Evansville, IN

Toss this simple recipe into the slow cooker first thing in the morning.
Hardly any prep is required! Leftovers freeze well too.

3 boneless, skinless chicken
   breasts
15-oz. can corn, drained
15-oz. can black beans, drained
   and rinsed

8-oz. jar salsa
1 onion, coarsely chopped
8-oz. pkg. cream cheese, cubed
taco shells or tortilla chips

Place chicken breasts in a slow cooker. Top with corn, beans, salsa
and onion. Cover and cook on low setting for 6 to 8 hours, until
chicken is tender. About 30 minutes before serving, shred chicken in
slow cooker. Add the cream cheese; stir to combine. Cover and cook
on low setting for 30 minutes, or until cream cheese has melted. Serve
chicken mixture with taco shells or tortilla chips. Makes 8 servings.

Set a regular dinner theme for each night and it'll be a snap to
make out your shopping list. Some tasty, budget-friendly
themes are Italian Night, Soup & Salad Night and Chili Night...
your family is sure to think of other favorites too!

Ham & Scalloped Potatoes

Eileen Bennett
Jenison, MI

Leftover ham from Sunday dinner? This is my family's favorite leftover type of recipe!

6 to 8 slices cooked ham,
   divided
8 to 10 potatoes, peeled, thinly
   sliced and divided
2 onions, thinly sliced and
   divided

salt and pepper to taste
1 c. shredded Cheddar cheese,
   divided
10-3/4 oz. can cream of
   mushroom soup
paprika to taste

In a slow cooker, layer half each of ham, potatoes and onions. Season with salt and pepper; sprinkle with half of cheese. Repeat layering. Spoon soup over top; sprinkle with paprika. Cover and cook on low setting for 8 to 10 hours, or on high setting for 4 hours. Makes 4 to 6 servings.

A flexible plastic cutting mat makes speedy work of slicing & dicing...after chopping, just fold it in half and pour ingredients into the mixing bowl. Keep two mats on hand for chopping meat and veggies separately.

Cabbage & Pork Chops

Trella Ary
Hornbeak, TN

Sure is good to come home to this meal on a cold and busy day!

4 c. cabbage, shredded
2 apples, peeled, cored and
   coarsely chopped
1 onion, chopped
1/3 c. brown sugar, packed
1/2 c. cider vinegar

1/2 c. apple juice
1 t. salt, divided
3 lbs. boneless pork chops,
   fat trimmed
1/4 t. pepper
1 T. oil

In a 5-quart slow cooker, combine cabbage, apples, onion, brown sugar, vinegar, juice and 1/2 teaspoon salt. Mix well and set aside. Sprinkle pork chops with remaining salt and pepper. Heat oil in a large skillet over medium heat; add pork chops and brown on both sides. Arrange pork chops over cabbage mixture; cover and cook on low setting for 6 hours, or until pork chops are fork-tender. Makes 6 servings.

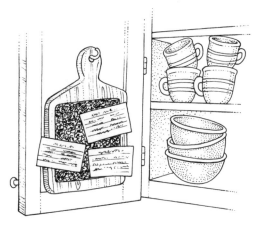

Keep most-used recipes at your fingertips! Tack them to self-stick cork tiles placed inside a kitchen cabinet door.

Kickin' Pork Chops

Amy Woods
Collinsville, TX

I love these quick & easy chops! My son Stephen puts them on when he gets home from high school. I simply add sides like boiled new potatoes and steamed Brussels sprouts for a healthy weeknight meal we enjoy.

4 to 6 thick-cut boneless
    pork chops
10-3/4 oz. can cream of
    chicken soup

1-oz. pkg ranch salad
    dressing mix
1 T. Creole seasoning

Spray a slow cooker with non-stick cooking spray. Lay pork chops in slow cooker and set aside. Mix remaining ingredients in a bowl; spoon over pork chops. Cover and cook on low setting for 4 to 5 hours, until pork chops are tender. Makes 4 to 6 servings.

A clear plastic over-the-door shoe organizer is super for pantry storage...just slip gravy mix packets, spice jars and other small items into the pockets.

BBQ Pork Chops

Diane Smith
Burlington, NJ

*Pair with potato salad and sweet corn for a
delicious midwinter picnic.*

18-oz. bottle barbecue sauce,
   divided
8 thick-cut bone-in pork chops,
   divided

1 to 2 onions, thickly sliced,
   separated into rings and
   divided

Spray a slow cooker with non-stick vegetable spray. Spread a thin layer of barbecue sauce in bottom of slow cooker. Alternately layer pork chops and onion slices with barbecue sauce; pour remaining sauce over top. Cover and cook on high setting setting on low setting for 7 to 8 hours, or on high setting for 3 to 4 hours, until pork chops are very tender. Makes 8 servings.

The ceramic crock in a slow cooker may crack if exposed to sudden temperature changes. Don't set a hot crock directly on a cold counter; always put a tea towel down first. Likewise, don't put a crock straight from the refrigerator into a preheated base.

Spaghetti Pie

Vickie

*An old favorite! Sometimes I layer sliced mushrooms
and black olives with the other ingredients.*

8-oz. pkg. spaghetti, uncooked
  and broken up
1 lb. ground beef
32-oz. jar pasta sauce
2 eggs, beaten

1/3 c. grated Parmesan cheese
3 c. cottage cheese, divided
1 c. shredded Italian-blend
  cheese, divided

Cook spaghetti according to package directions, just until tender; drain
and return to pan. Meanwhile, brown beef in a skillet over medium
heat; drain. Add sauce to beef; simmer over low heat for several
minutes. To spaghetti in pan, add eggs and Parmesan cheese; stir
gently to mix. Spoon 1/2 cup sauce mixture into a slow cooker. Layer
with half each of spaghetti mixture, cottage cheese, remaining sauce
mixture and shredded cheese. Repeat layering. Cover and cook on low
setting for 6 to 8 hours. Makes 6 servings.

Bake some savory garlic twists for dinner. Separate refrigerated
bread stick dough and lay flat on an ungreased baking sheet. Brush
with olive oil; sprinkle with garlic salt and dried parsley. Give each
bread stick a twist or two and bake as directed on the package.

Slow-Cooker Rigatoni Pizza

Meg Swearingen
Antioch, IL

I made this recipe for my parents...we all love it!

16-oz. pkg. rigatoni pasta, uncooked and divided
1-1/2 lbs. ground Italian pork sausage
1 onion, chopped
1 orange pepper, chopped and divided

1/2 lb. sliced mushrooms, divided
3-oz. pkg. sliced pepperoni, divided
15-oz. jar pizza sauce, divided
16-oz. pkg. shredded mozzarella cheese, divided

Cook half of the package of pasta according to package directions; drain. Reserve uncooked pasta for use in another recipe. While pasta cooks, brown sausage with onion in a skillet over medium heat; drain. In a slow cooker, layer half each of sausage mixture, pepper, pasta, mushrooms, pepperoni, pizza sauce and cheese. Repeat layers. Cover and cook on low setting for 3 to 4 hours, until hot and bubbly. Makes 6 to 8 servings.

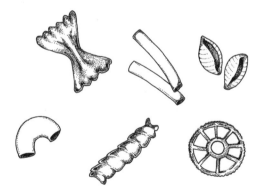

Pasta that will be added to a slow cooker can be cooked for the shortest time indicated on the package. It will become tender while the dish simmers.

Green Chile Mac & Cheese

Marian Buckley
Fontana, CA

A good old stand-by with a little extra zip! Use your favorite tube-shaped pasta or elbow macaroni.

2 c. mostaccioli pasta, uncooked
2 T. butter
8-oz. pkg. pasteurized process
   cheese, cubed
8-oz. pkg. cream cheese, cubed
1 t. Dijon mustard

12-oz. can evaporated milk
1 c. milk
1/2 c. whipping cream
2 10-oz. cans diced tomatoes
   with green chiles

Spray a 4-quart slow cooker with non-stick vegetable spray. Add uncooked pasta and remaining ingredients except tomatoes. Stir until well combined. Cover and cook on low setting for 4 hours, or until pasta is tender and cheese is bubbly. Shortly before serving time, stir in tomatoes with juice. Cover and cook for several more minutes, until heated through. Makes 6 servings.

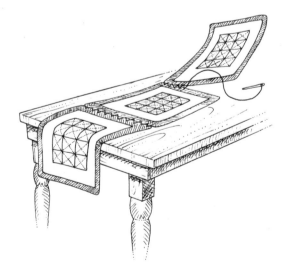

Whip up a country-style table runner in a jiffy! Just stitch several quilted placemats end-to-end.

Chili Sans Carne

Amanda Black
Carterville, GA

At my local ladies' gym, we had a challenge to create a recipe that was high in healthy flavor and low in salt. I adapted my old meat- and fat-filled recipe to make it healthier and meatless...it's a winner!

2 15-oz. cans no-sodium-added black beans, drained and rinsed
15-oz. can no-sodium added kidney beans, drained and rinsed
15-oz. can corn, drained and rinsed
14-1/2 oz. can diced tomatoes
6-oz. can tomato paste
1/2 c. onion, chopped
2 cloves garlic, chopped
Garnish: thinly sliced green onions
low-sodium whole wheat crackers

Combine beans and corn in a slow cooker. Add tomatoes with juice, tomato paste, onion and garlic. Cover and cook on low setting for 8 hours. Garnish with green onions; serve with crackers. Makes 8 servings.

Mix up your own flavorful salsa. Combine one 14-1/2 ounce can of diced tomatoes and green chiles, 1/2 cup diced onion, a minced garlic clove and a tablespoon of lime juice. Enjoy it chunky style, or for a smoother consistency, place in a food processor and pulse several times.

Tamale Casserole

Carolyn Deckard
Bedford, IN

*Another easy meal you can put together and let cook while
you work or play. I always serve a lettuce salad with it.*

1 lb. ground beef
1 egg, beaten
1-1/2 c. milk
3/4 c. cornmeal
14-1/2 can diced tomatoes
15-1/4 oz. can corn, drained

2-1/2 oz. can sliced black olives,
    drained
1-oz. pkg. chili seasoning mix
1 t. seasoned salt
1 c. shredded Cheddar cheese

In a skillet over medium heat, cook beef until no longer pink; drain.
Meanwhile, in a bowl, combine egg, milk and cornmeal. Stir until
smooth; add tomatoes with juice, corn, olives, seasoning mix and
seasoned salt. Add beef; stir well and spoon into a greased slow
cooker. Cover and cook on high setting for 3 hours and 45 minutes.
Sprinkle with cheese. Cover and cook 15 minutes longer, or until
cheese is melted. Makes 6 servings.

Pick up some paper plates, cups and napkins in seasonal
designs...they'll make sandwich suppers fun when time
is short and clean-up will be a breeze.

Tex-Mex Enchiladas

Cassie Hooker
La Porte, TX

My family loves this dish! It's a great meal to serve on a cold night.

1 lb. lean ground beef
1 T. oil
1/2 c. onion, chopped
1 green pepper, chopped
15-oz. can ranch-style beans,
    drained and rinsed
10-oz. can diced tomatoes with
    green chiles, drained
1 t. chili powder

1/2 t. ground cumin
1/2 t. salt
1/4 t. pepper
1/4 t. garlic powder
8-oz. pkg. shredded Colby Jack
    cheese
8 flour tortillas, divided
15-oz. can red enchilada sauce

Cook beef in a large skillet over medium heat until browned; drain.
Meanwhile, in a separate skillet over medium heat, sauté onion and
green pepper in oil until tender. Add onion mixture to beef. Stir in
beans, tomatoes and seasonings. In a slow cooker, place 2 tortillas
side-by-side, overlapping if necessary. Layer with 1/4 of the beef
mixture and 1/4 of the cheese. Repeat layers 3 more times. Pour
enchilada sauce over top. Cover and cook on low setting for 2 to
2-1/2 hours, until heated through and cheese is melted. Makes
8 servings.

A speedy side for any south-of-the-border supper! Stir spicy
salsa and shredded cheese into hot cooked rice. Cover and
let stand a few minutes, until the cheese melts.

Slow-Cooked Posole

Tonya Sheppard
Galveston, TX

A down-home favorite from south of the border! Sometimes I use 2 pounds of boneless chicken cubes instead of the pork. Add a basket of warm flour tortillas and dinner is served.

1 T. oil
2-lb. pork loin roast, cut into
  1-inch cubes
2 14-1/2 oz. cans red and/or
  green enchilada sauce
2 to 3 15-1/2 oz. cans white
  and/or yellow hominy,
  drained
1 onion, sliced
4-oz. can diced green chiles

4 cloves garlic, minced
1/2 t. cayenne pepper, or to taste
2 t. dried oregano
1/4 c. fresh cilantro, chopped
1/2 t. salt
Garnish: shredded cabbage,
  sliced green onions,
  shredded Mexican-blend
  cheese, lime wedges

Heat oil in a large skillet over high heat. Add pork and brown on all sides, about 5 minutes; drain. Place pork in a 4-quart slow cooker. Top with sauce, hominy, onion, chiles, garlic, cayenne pepper and oregano. Add water to fill slow cooker 2/3 full; stir gently. Cover and cook on high setting for 6 to 7 hours. Turn slow cooker to low setting; stir in cilantro and salt. Cover and cook for an additional 30 minutes. To serve, spoon into soup bowls; serve with desired garnishes. Makes 8 servings.

Jot down all your favorite, tried & true slow-cooker recipes for a new bride who's just learning to cook. Tuck them inside a brand new slow cooker...she'll love 'em both!

Beckie's Pinto Beans

Beckie Apple
Grannis, AR

My family grew up eating Momma's pinto beans that simmered for hours on the stove...but thank goodness someone invented the slow cooker! Serve with hot cornbread for a simple and satisfying meal.

1 lb. dried pinto beans, rinsed
    and sorted
6 slices bacon, cut into 2-inch
    pieces

1-oz. pkg. onion soup mix
6 c. hot water
1/4 t. salt
1/4 t. pepper

Combine dried beans, bacon and soup mix in a 4-quart slow cooker; stir well. Add water, salt and pepper; stir again. Cover and cook on low setting for 8 hours, or on high setting for 4 to 5 hours, until beans are tender. Add more water as needed to keep water level one inch above the beans. Makes 8 servings.

Freeze mashed, fresh avocado to keep on hand for quick guacamole. Just add 1/2 teaspoon of lime or lemon juice per avocado, mix well and store in a plastic zipping bag, making sure to remove all the air before sealing. Thaw in the refrigerator before using.

Creamy Dreamy Chicken

Dina Willard
Abingdon, MD

I love to feed my family delicious meals to warm their tummies and their hearts. It's especially nice to know that at the end of a long day, dinner is ready. We can relax and share our stories of the day.

5 to 6 boneless, skinless chicken
   thighs
2-1/2 lbs. new redskin potatoes
   or Yukon Gold potatoes,
   halved
salt and pepper to taste
10-oz. pkg. frozen carrots,
   thawed

1/2 c. green onions, thinly sliced
1 bunch asparagus, trimmed and
   cut into thirds
2 10-3/4 oz. cans cream of
   mushroom soup
1/2 c. unsweetened almond milk
   or low-fat milk

In a slow cooker, layer chicken and potatoes; season with salt and pepper. Add carrots and green onions, mixing gently; place asparagus on top. Add more salt and pepper, if desired. Whisk together soup and milk in a bowl; pour over top. Cover and cook on low setting for 7 to 8 hours. Serves 4.

A crisp green salad goes well with all kinds of dinners. For a zippy citrus dressing, shake up 1/2 cup olive oil, 1/3 cup lemon or orange juice and a tablespoon of Dijon mustard in a small jar and chill to blend.

"Rotisserie" Chicken

Ann Mathis
Biscoe, AR

I use to buy deli roast chicken at my local grocery store. Then I found this recipe and it is so easy and so good. You can adjust any of the seasonings as you like. Wow, how simple is that?

3 to 4-lb. broiler chicken
2 T. paprika
2 T. garlic powder, or 3 cloves
   garlic, minced
1-1/2 t. onion powder

1 t. salt
1/2 t. pepper
Optional: 1/2 t. cayenne pepper
3 to 4 t. water

Spray a slow cooker with non-stick vegetable spray. Add chicken breast-side up. In a small bowl, combine remaining ingredients except water; stir in water by teaspoonfuls until a paste forms. Coat chicken inside and out with paste. Cover and cook on low setting for 6 to 7 hours, or on high setting for 3-1/2 to 4-1/2 hours, until a meat thermometer inserted in thickest part of the thigh registers 180 degrees. Remove to a platter; let stand several minutes before slicing. Makes 6 servings.

Try roasting veggies in the slow cooker...so simple! Just drizzle with a couple tablespoons of olive oil and season to taste. Cook on high setting for about 3 hours, stirring occasionally. Delicious!

Chicken Cacciatore

Sandra Monroe
Preston, MD

My husband loves this meal. It's so simple to put together and a good way to use fresh summer vegetables.

4 boneless, skinless chicken
   breasts
26-oz. jar chunky garden-style
   pasta sauce
1 zucchini, chopped
1 green pepper, chopped

1 c. onion, chopped
cooked wide egg noodles
   or spaghetti
Garnish: grated Parmesan
   cheese

Spray a slow cooker with non-stick vegetable spray. Add chicken breasts; pour pasta sauce over chicken. Top with vegetables. Cover and cook on low setting for 6 to 8 hours. Serve chicken with sauce mixture from slow cooker, spooned over cooked noodles or spaghetti. Garnish with cheese. Makes 4 servings.

Use a vegetable peeler to quickly cut thin curls from a block of Parmesan cheese for garnishing pasta dishes.

Pasta Sauce à la Carmela

Carmela Seagull
Ontario, Canada

Coming from an Italian family, pasta sauce is a staple for me. It's very versatile and you can use it in many dishes. When we were young we would pick the fresh tomatoes from the farm...a very fond memory for me. Serve this sauce over pasta or add it to chicken.

2 c. sweet onion, chopped
6 cloves garlic, chopped
2 T. olive oil
4 28-oz. cans whole tomatoes
6 leaves fresh basil, torn
3 cubes chicken bouillon

2 t. sugar
1 bay leaf
salt and pepper to taste
Garnish: shredded Parmesan
  cheese

In a skillet over medium heat, sauté onion and garlic in oil until onion is softened. Transfer mixture to a slow cooker; add tomatoes in juice and remaining ingredients except cheese. Cover and cook on low setting for 6 to 8 hours, or on high setting for 2 to 4 hours. Discard bay leaf before serving. Serve sauce as desired, topped with Parmesan cheese. Makes 8 servings.

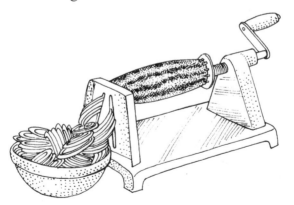

For a healthy change from regular pasta, make "noodles" from zucchini or summer squash. Cut the squash into long, thin strips with a sharp knife or use a spiral vegetable cutter to create thin strands. Steam lightly or sauté in a little olive oil and toss with your favorite pasta sauce.

Schnitzel Beans

Karen Dennis
Mount Vernon, OH

*My mom used to make this for our family get-togethers. She says
the recipes was probably started by my great-grandma. You'll
know it's the right amount of vinegar when your eyes water!*

1/4 lb. bacon
1 onion, chopped
1/2 c. sugar

1/4 c. to 1/2 c. cider vinegar
8 c. fresh green beans, trimmed

In a skillet over medium heat, cook bacon until crisp. Remove bacon to
a paper towel, reserving drippings in skillet. Allow drippings to cool
slightly; add onion, sugar and 1/4 cup vinegar. Cook until sugar is
dissolved, onion is tender and vinegar aroma is strong. Transfer beans
to a slow cooker; cover with vinegar mixture. Add remaining vinegar,
if desired. Cover and cook on low setting for 4 to 5 hours, or on high
setting for 2 to 3 hours. Garnish with crumbled bacon. Makes 6 to
8 servings.

Sweet-and-Sour Red Cabbage

Megan Brooks
Antioch, TN

*My Grandma Studer used to make a version of this. It's an
old-fashioned side that's good with grilled sausages.*

4 slices bacon, diced
1/4 c. brown sugar, packed
2 T. all-purpose flour
1/4 c. cider vinegar
1/4 c. water

1/2 t. salt
1/8 t. pepper
1 head red cabbage, shredded
1/4 c. onion, finely chopped

In a skillet, cook bacon until crisp. Drain and refrigerate bacon,
reserving one tablespoon drippings. In a bowl, combine reserved
drippings, flour, vinegar, water and seasonings; stir until smooth. Place
cabbage and onion in a slow cooker. Pour mixture over top; toss to
mix well. Cover and cook on low setting for 6 to 7 hours, until cabbage
is tender. Serve warm, topped with reserved bacon. Serves 6 to 8.

Serbian Kielbasa & Sauerkraut

Anna Hessel
Elmwood Park, IL

This delicious recipe was handed down from my Serbian great-grandmother. A slow cooker makes this an easy favorite.

3 14-1/2 oz. cans sauerkraut,
 partially drained
28-oz. can stewed tomatoes
1 onion, sliced
1/2 c. water

2 14-oz. pkgs. Kielbasa
 sausage, cut into 1-inch
 pieces
paprika and pepper to taste

To a slow cooker, add sauerkraut, tomatoes with juice, onion and water. Cover and cook on high setting while preparing sausage. Meanwhile, in a skillet over medium-high heat, cook sausage until browned on all sides. Drain; season with paprika and pepper. Add sausage to mixture in slow cooker; stir. Cover and cook on high setting for 2 hours, stirring often. Makes 8 servings.

"Adopt" an older neighbor as a grandparent. Include him or her in the children's ball games and family outings... share stories over dinner. Your family can help out by weeding flower beds, raking leaves and running errands... it's sure to be rewarding for everybody!

Black-Eyed Peas & Ham Hock

Amy Butcher
Columbus, GA

Down-home goodness! We like it spicy, but if you don't, there are lots of other tasty flavors of diced tomatoes to choose from.

6 c. water
1 lb. dried black-eyed peas,
   rinsed and sorted
14-1/2 oz. can diced tomatoes
   with green chiles
14-1/2 oz. can diced tomatoes
   with jalapeño peppers

2 10-1/2 oz. cans chicken broth
1 stalk celery, chopped
salt and pepper to taste
1 ham hock

In a large saucepan over high heat, bring water to a boil. Add peas and return to a full boil; boil for 2 minutes. Remove from heat; let stand for one hour. Drain, discarding water. Add peas to a slow cooker. Stir in tomatoes with juice and remaining ingredients, pushing ham hock down into ingredients. Cover and cook on low setting for 8 to 10 hours, until peas are tender. Makes 10 to 12 servings.

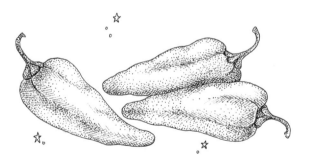

Fresh hot peppers from your own garden or a nearby farmers' market are extra flavorful, but take care when slicing them. It's best to wear rubber gloves, and be sure not to touch your eyes.

Savory Corn Spoonbread

Annette Ingram
Grand Rapids, MI

Country-style flavor, so easy to fix.

1 c. yellow cornmeal
2 t. baking powder
2 eggs, beaten
1 c. buttermilk
2 T. oil

14-3/4 oz. can creamed corn
1 c. shredded sharp Cheddar
  cheese
Optional: 1 T. canned diced
  green chiles

In a bowl, beat together all ingredients. Pour batter into a greased 4-quart slow cooker. Cover and cook on low setting for 4 hours, or until a toothpick inserted in the center tests clean. Serve warm. Serves 4 to 6.

Cilantro Green Beans

Beverley Williams
San Antonio, TX

My favorite way to fix green beans! I don't care for the ones with all the bacon and salt.

4 c. fresh green beans, trimmed
1 tomato, diced

1/4 c. onion, diced
1 T. dried cilantro

Place beans, tomato and onion in a slow cooker. Cover with water, filling slow cooker 2/3 full. Cover and cook on high setting for 10 to 12 hours. When beans are almost tender, add cilantro. Cover and cook on high setting for 30 minutes longer. Makes 6 to 8 servings.

It's a lovely thing...everyone sitting down together, sharing food.

- Alice May Brock

Crock-a-dile Ribs

Adam Gelbard
Honolulu, HI

When my two boys Kai and Keanu were growing up, to get them interested in new foods we always gave interesting names to dishes. One example was "turtle tails" for green beans. This is a great, easy recipe for barbecue ribs.

2 to 3 lbs. pork spareribs, cut
    into serving-size sections
2 c. cola
1 sweet onion, sliced
1 t. garlic powder

1 t. salt
1 t. pepper
1/4 t. cayenne pepper
favorite barbecue sauce to taste

Remove silver skin from the underside of chilled spareribs; place ribs in a slow cooker. Combine cola, onion and seasonings in a bowl; mix well and spoon over ribs. Cover and cook on low setting for 6 to 8 hours, or until ribs are very tender. Remove ribs to a serving platter; drain liquid in slow cooker. Coat with desired amount of barbecue sauce just before serving. Makes 4 to 5 servings.

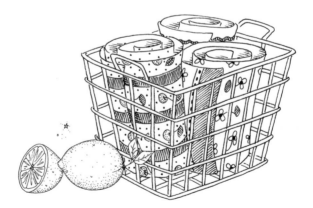

Set out a basket of rolled-up washcloths, moistened with lemon-scented water and warmed briefly in the microwave. Sure to be appreciated when yummy-but-messy foods like barbecued ribs and fried chicken are on the menu!

Maple Whiskey Ribs

Staci Allen
Sheboygan, WI

We are always given fresh maple syrup around the holidays. Our family is not into breakfast, so we enjoy using the syrup in different meat dishes. Enjoy these ribs with buttered noodles or warm bread.

1/2 c. pure maple syrup
1/4 c. whiskey or fruit juice
2 T. Dijon mustard

2 lbs. pork spareribs, cut into
   serving-size sections
1 large purple onion, sliced

In a small bowl, whisk together syrup, whiskey or juice and mustard. Brush mixture over spareribs. Place ribs in a slow cooker; top with onion slices. Cover and cook on low setting for 6 to 8 hours, until ribs are very tender. Makes 4 servings.

If you prefer grilled ribs, just place slow-cooked meat on
a broiler pan...pop under the broiler for a few minutes,
until they're slightly char-broiled and crisp.

Laurie's Baked Ziti

Laurie Davis
Eatontown, NJ

When my oven broke, it was a challenge to make dinner for my family. We love comfort foods and my family loves my baked ziti. I figured if it can be done in the oven, it can be done in a slow cooker! So after trying it a couple different times, here is what I came up with. I serve this with a tossed salad and warm Italian bread.

16-oz. pkg. ziti pasta, uncooked
1-1/2 lbs. ground beef
1/2 t. dried, chopped onion and
   garlic seasoning
1/2 t. Italian seasoning

salt and pepper to taste
16-oz. container ricotta cheese
32-oz. jar pasta sauce, divided
16-oz. pkg. shredded mozzarella
   cheese, divided

Cook spaghetti according to package directions, just until tender; drain. Meanwhile, in a skillet over medium heat, combine beef and seasonings. Cook until beef is no longer pink; drain. In a large bowl, combine beef mixture, ricotta cheese and a small amount of sauce; mix well until mixture looks creamy. Spray a 5-quart slow cooker with non-stick vegetable spray. Pour just enough of remaining sauce into slow cooker to cover the bottom. Transfer half of the pasta into the slow cooker. Top pasta with half each of beef mixture, remaining sauce and mozzarella cheese. Repeat layering. Cover and cook on low setting for 3 to 4 hours, until hot and bubbly. Serves 6.

Make a fresh-tasting side dish for pasta. Combine 3 to 4 sliced zucchini, 1/2 teaspoon minced garlic and a tablespoon of chopped fresh basil. Sauté in a little olive oil until tender.

Bowties with Sausage & Mushrooms

Nancy Wise
Little Rock, AR

A hearty dish that's perfect for Sunday dinners.

3/4 lb. Italian ground
   pork sausage
1/2 c. onion, chopped
2 cloves garlic, minced
28-oz. can crushed tomatoes
8-oz. can tomato sauce
6-oz. can tomato paste
2 c. sliced mushrooms

2/3 c. water
1 T. sugar
1 t. dried rosemary
1/4 t. pepper
12-oz. pkg. bowtie pasta,
   cooked
Garnish: grated Parmesan
   cheese

In a skillet over medium heat, brown sausage with onion. Drain; place in a slow cooker. Add tomatoes with juice, tomato sauce, tomato paste, mushrooms, water, sugar and seasonings; stir. Cover and cook on low setting for 6 to 8 hours. Stir. Serve over cooked pasta, sprinkled with Parmesan cheese. Makes 6 to 8 servings.

Cook up perfect pasta. Fill a large pot with water and bring to a rolling boil. Add a tablespoon of salt, if desired. Stir in pasta; return to a rolling boil. Boil, uncovered, for the time recommended on package. No need to add oil...stirring frequently will keep pasta from sticking together.

Angela's Simple Sauce & Sausages

Joanne Curran
Arlington, MA

This recipe was originally given to me by Angela, my closest friend, and it was a hit. My family loves it! If you don't care for hot sausages, just use two packages of sweet Italian sausages.

1 lb. sweet Italian pork
    sausage links
1 lb. hot Italian pork sausage
    links
2 28-oz. cans crushed tomatoes

16-oz. pkg. ziti or other pasta,
    cooked
Garnish: grated Parmesan
    cheese

Cut sausage links apart, if necessary; add to a slow cooker. Add undrained tomatoes. Cover and cook on low setting for 6 hours, or until sausage is cooked through. Top cooked pasta with sausage links; ladle sauce over top. Sprinkle with cheese. Makes 6 servings.

Mix up some zesty oil & vinegar salad dressing. Combine 3/4 cup olive oil, 1/4 cup white wine vinegar, 3/4 teaspoon salt and 1/4 teaspoon pepper in a small jar. Add some minced garlic, if you like. Shake well; keep refrigerated.

Christa's Mac & Cheese

Theda Light
Christiansburg, VA

This recipe was given to me by my friend Christa, who is a great cook. It's creamy and satisfying...real comfort food.

8-oz. pkg. elbow macaroni,
   uncooked
3 T. butter, sliced
2 T. oil
2 T. onion, minced

1/4 t. salt
2 to 3 c. pasteurized process
   cheese, cubed
1 c. shredded Cheddar cheese
3 c. milk

Cook macaroni according to package directions; drain. Meanwhile, combine butter, oil, onion and salt in a large bowl. Pour cooked macaroni over ingredients in bowl; mix well. Spoon macaroni mixture into a greased 4-quart slow cooker. Add cheese and milk; stir well. Cover and cook on low setting for 3 to 4 hours. Stir occasionally. Makes 5 to 6 servings.

If you like crispy crumb toppings, try this. Melt one tablespoon butter in a skillet over medium-high heat. Add one cup bread crumbs or crushed crackers; cook and stir until toasty. Add garlic powder, salt and pepper to taste. Sprinkle crumbs over individual servings.

125

BBQ Short Ribs

Claire Bertram
Lexington, KY

This is a great recipe! It just takes a little of this & a little of that, which you probably already have on hand, and a few minutes to put it all together.

2 to 3 lbs. beef short ribs
1/2 c. tomato, chopped
1/2 c. onion, chopped
1/3 c. water
1/4 c. tomato paste
3 T. brown sugar, packed
1 T. mustard

2 t. seasoned salt
2 t. cider vinegar
1 t. beef bouillon granules
1 t. Worcestershire sauce
1 T. cornstarch
1 T. cold water

Combine ribs, tomato and onion in a slow cooker; set aside. Combine remaining ingredients except cornstarch and cold water in a bowl. Mix well; spoon mixture over ribs and turn to coat. Cover and cook on low setting for 6 to 7 hours, until ribs are very tender. In a small bowl, stir together cornstarch and cold water until smooth; gradually stir into juices in slow cooker. Cover and cook on high setting for 10 to 15 minutes, until sauce is thickened. Makes 4 servings.

If a recipe calls for just a partial can of tomato paste, spoon the rest into ice cube trays and freeze for later use.

Laurie's Mom's Baked Beans

Kathy Grashoff
Fort Wayne, IN

This is my sister-in-law's mom's recipe. It is the only recipe I use for baked beans. Her mom is gone now, but her recipe lives on!

2 32-oz. cans Great Northern
   beans, most of liquid drained
1 onion, chopped
1-1/2 c. to 2 c. catsup

1/2 c. brown sugar, packed,
   or more to taste
6 slices bacon, chopped

In a slow cooker sprayed with non-stick vegetable spray, combine beans and onion. Stir in 1-1/2 cups catsup, adding more as necessary until mixture looks juicy. Add brown sugar to taste. Stir in bacon. Cover and cook on low setting for 6 to 8 hours, until thickened and bubbly. Makes 6 to 8 servings.

If you like sweet cornbread, you'll love this family-size recipe. Mix together an 8-1/2 ounce box of corn muffin mix, a 9-ounce box of yellow cake mix, 1/2 cup water, 1/3 cup milk and 2 beaten eggs. Pour into a greased 13"x9" baking pan and bake at 350 degrees for 15 to 20 minutes. Scrumptious!

Creamy Chicken & Veggies

Shirley Howie
Foxboro, MA

This is a fabulous one-pot dinner that only takes about 15 minutes to prepare. I like to serve it with hot biscuits or rolls to soak up the delicious gravy!

1 onion, diced
6 new redskin potatoes,
   quartered
2 c. carrots, peeled and sliced
1 c. sliced mushrooms
2 lbs. boneless, skinless
   chicken thighs

10-3/4 oz. pkg. cream of
   mushroom soup
2/3 c. chicken broth
1/4 c. all-purpose flour
1-oz. pkg. onion soup mix
1/2 t. poultry seasoning
1/2 t. dried thyme

Combine vegetables in a 5-quart slow cooker; arrange chicken thighs over vegetables. Stir together remaining ingredients in a bowl; spoon over chicken. Cover and cook on low setting for 4 to 5 hours, until chicken juices run clear when pierced. Makes 4 to 6 servings.

Keep the kids happy while dinner simmers in the slow cooker.
Line the table with kraft paper, pull out the crayons and
let 'em decorate the "tablecloth" any way they choose!

Chicken in a Crock

Sandy Coffey
Cincinnati, OH

A favorite one-pot family meal whenever we get together for board game night. It's warm, hearty and easy to dish up. Add a basket of hot rolls and a tossed salad...game's on!

1/4 c. all-purpose flour
1-1/2 lbs. boneless, skinless
   chicken breasts, cubed
1-1/2 c. frozen crinkle-style
   carrots

1/2 c. onion, chopped
14-oz. can chicken broth
1 c. frozen peas
1/2 c. cream cheese, softened

Place flour in a shallow dish. Coat chicken in flour and add to a slow cooker. Add carrots and onion; pour in broth. Cover and cook on low setting for 6 to 8 hours, until chicken juices run clear. About 30 minutes before serving, stir in peas and cream cheese. Cover and cook on low setting another 30 minutes; stir again. Makes 4 to 6 servings.

While supper simmers in the slow cooker, there's time to do other things. Why not bake up a double batch of cookies? There will be plenty for dessert and extras to share with a neighbor, babysitter or anyone else who would love to know you're thinking of them.

Cashew Chicken

Anne Alesauskas
Minocqua, WI

This is one of the simplest recipes in my recipe box and I think you'll love it! We just love Chinese food...unfortunately, our options aren't great for take-out, so I make my own whenever possible. Using the slow cooker is an added bonus on those days when you're running like mad.

1/2 c. all-purpose flour
1/8 t. pepper
2 lbs. boneless, skinless chicken
    breasts, cubed
2 T. canola oil
1/4 c. soy sauce
2 T. rice wine vinegar
2 T. catsup

1 T. brown sugar, packed
1 clove garlic, minced
1/2 t. fresh ginger, peeled
    and grated
red pepper flakes to taste
cooked brown rice
Garnish: 1/2 c. cashews

Combine flour and pepper in a plastic zipping bag. Add chicken pieces to bag; toss to coat and set aside. Heat oil in a large skillet over medium-high heat. Cook chicken for about 5 minutes, until golden on all sides but not cooked through. Transfer chicken to a slow cooker; set aside. In a small bowl, combine remaining ingredients except rice and cashews. Pour mixture over chicken, stirring slightly. Cover and cook on low setting for 3 to 4 hours, or on high setting for one to 2 hours, until chicken juices run clear. To serve, spoon chicken mixture over cooked rice; top with cashews. Makes 4 servings.

Cut beef, chicken or pork into thin strips or slices in a snap!
Just freeze for 20 to 30 minutes before slicing.

Sweet-and-Sour Chicken

Maryalice Dobbert
King George, VA

This makes a delicious meal without all the fuss...it just tastes like you went to a lot of effort!

5 to 6 boneless, skinless chicken
    breasts
1 green pepper, cut into chunks
1 onion, cut into chunks
15-oz. can pineapple chunks,
    drained and juice reserved

16-oz. jar tangy barbecue sauce
2 T. Worcestershire sauce
Optional: 1 T. cornstarch
soy sauce, salt and pepper
    to taste
cooked rice

In a slow cooker, combine chicken breasts, green pepper, onion and pineapple. Top with sauces. Cover and cook on low setting for 6 to 7 hours. Remove chicken to a plate; shred and set aside. If a thicker sauce consistency is desired, remove one cup of cooking liquid to a bowl. Mix well with reserved pineapple juice; stir in cornstarch and pour mixture back into slow cooker. Stir continuously on low setting until thickened slightly. Add shredded chicken to slow cooker and stir to combine. Season with soy sauce, salt and pepper. Serve chicken mixture over cooked rice. Makes 6 servings.

For a tasty change from rice, serve Asian-inspired dishes over rice noodles or thin spaghetti, or a bed of no-cooking-needed crispy chow mein noodles.

Cheesy Chicken

Jenifer Rutland
Hiawatha, KS

Slow-cooker meals are always the easiest for me. This one is a hit with the kids! The chicken is very tender and juicy. I serve it with mashed potatoes and use the cheesy sauce as a gravy.

6 to 8 boneless, skinless chicken breasts
1/2 c. butter, melted
10-3/4 oz. can cream of chicken soup
8-oz. container sour cream
1 onion, chopped
1 c. shredded Colby Jack cheese
salt and pepper to taste
8-oz. pkg. pasteurized process cheese, cubed

Place chicken in a slow cooker; drizzle with butter and set aside. In a bowl, combine soup, sour cream, onion, shredded cheese, salt and pepper. Mix well and pour over chicken. Add just enough water to cover ingredients. Add cheese cubes on top. Cover and cook on low setting for 6 to 8 hours. Makes 6 to 8 servings.

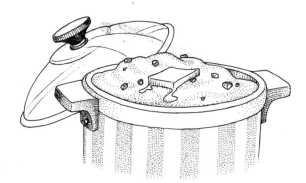

Everyone knows mashed potatoes are the perfect side dish for comfort-food dinners. Try a delicious secret the next time you make them...substitute equal parts chicken broth and cream for the milk. So flavorful!

Creamy Italian Chicken & Noodles

Lynda Willoughby
Fort Mill, SC

This recipe is very easy and kid-friendly, yet delicious enough for company. Just dress it up with a sprinkle of chopped fresh parsley.

6 boneless, skinless chicken
  thighs
2 1-oz. pkgs. zesty Italian salad
  dressing mix
32-oz. container chicken broth

2 8-oz. pkgs. cream cheese,
  cubed
16-oz. pkg. medium egg
  noodles, cooked

Place chicken thighs in a slow cooker. Sprinkle with dressing mix; pour broth over chicken. Cover and cook on low setting for 6 to 8 hours, until chicken is very tender. Remove chicken to a plate, reserving broth in slow cooker; shred chicken with a fork and set aside. Add cream cheese to broth in slow cooker; stir until melted. Add cooked noodles and shredded chicken to slow cooker; stir gently. Let stand for about 15 minutes, until thickened and creamy. Makes 6 servings.

Make meals extra special for your family! Pull out the good china and light some candles...you'll be making memories together.

Help-Yourself Hamburger Casserole

Eileen Bennett
Jenison, MI

Dinner is in the crock! This busy-day recipe is packed with healthy beef and vegetables. Everyone can fix their own plates while Mom is on the road, shuttling kids back & forth to school activities.

1-1/2 lbs. lean ground beef
2 potatoes, peeled and sliced
1 to 3 carrots, peeled and sliced
15-oz. can peas, well drained
3 onions, sliced

2 stalks celery, sliced
salt and pepper to taste
10-3/4 oz. can tomato soup
1-1/4 c. water

Brown beef in a skillet over medium heat; drain and set aside. Meanwhile, in a slow cooker, layer vegetables in order given; season each layer with salt and pepper. Add beef on top of celery. Whisk together soup and water in a bowl; pour into slow cooker. Cover and cook on low setting for 6 to 8 hours, or on high setting for 2 to 4 hours, stirring occasionally. Makes 4 servings.

Create a cozy corner for yourself with a comfy chair and a small table. With dinner simmering in a slow cooker, you'll have a quiet place to read a book, write in a journal or just enjoy a catnap before dinner.

Sandra's Swiss Steak

Sandra Monroe
Preston, MD

A really tasty recipe that's easy to fix before going to work...
ready to serve when you get home.

3 to 4 T. all-purpose flour
1-1/2 t. dry mustard
1/2 t. salt
1/4 t. pepper
1-1/2 to 2 lbs. beef round steak,
   cut into serving-size pieces

1 T. oil
1/2 c. onion, sliced
1 c. carrots, peeled and sliced
14-1/2 oz. can diced tomatoes
1-1/2 T. Worcestershire sauce
1 T. brown sugar, packed

Combine flour and seasonings in a shallow dish. Dredge steak pieces in flour mixture; set aside. Heat oil in a large skillet over medium heat; brown beef on both sides. Drain; remove to a slow cooker. Add onion and carrots to slow cooker. To the same skillet, add tomatoes with juice, Worcestershire sauce and brown sugar; simmer over low heat for 2 minutes. Pour tomato mixture into slow cooker. Cover and cook on low setting heat for 8 hours, or on high setting for 3 to 5 hours, until beef is tender. Serves 4.

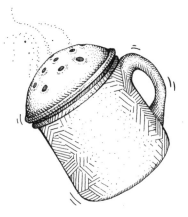

Keep a shaker canister of quick-mixing flour on hand
for dusting pork chops, cubes of stew beef or other
meat before browning.

Tex-Mex Beef & Beans

Lorrie Coop
Munday, TX

I love this recipe because it is so easy and delicious. It's great for lazy Sunday afternoons because I just toss everything in the slow cooker and curl up with a good book until it's ready to eat. Serve with your favorite cornbread.

3 lbs. stew beef cubes
2 c. dried pinto beans, rinsed
   and sorted
10-oz. can diced tomatoes and
   green chiles

8-oz. can tomato sauce
4-oz. can chopped green chiles
1 onion, chopped
1/4 c. sugar
salt and pepper to taste

Place beef cubes in a 6-quart slow cooker; add dried beans. Combine tomatoes with juice and remaining ingredients in a bowl; spoon into slow cooker. Add enough water to cover ingredients by 2 inches. Cover and and cook on high setting for 4 to 6 hours, until beef and beans are tender. Add hot water as needed during cooking to keep ingredients covered. Makes 6 to 8 servings.

Mix up your own chili powder blend. Fill a shaker with
2 teaspoons garlic powder, 2 teaspoons cumin and one teaspoon
each of cayenne pepper, paprika and oregano. Easy to adjust
to your own taste!

Sloppy Burritos

Kaela Oates
Waverly, WV

A must-have at our family get-togethers...there's always
someone new asking for the recipe!

4 to 5-lb. beef sirloin tip roast
1 c. water
2 1-oz. pkgs. taco seasoning
  mix
2 10-3/4 oz. cans cream of
  mushroom soup
16-oz. jar salsa
1 c. shredded Mexican-blend
  cheese

8-oz. container sour cream
12 to 16 burrito-size flour
  tortillas
Garnish: salsa, sour cream,
  shredded Mexican-blend
  cheese, shredded lettuce,
  diced tomato

Place roast in a large slow cooker. Pour in water; sprinkle with
seasoning mix. Cover and cook on low setting for 8 to 10 hours, until
beef is very tender. Shred beef in cooking liquid with 2 forks; keep
warm while preparing cheese sauce. In a saucepan, combine soup,
salsa and cheese. Cook over medium heat, stirring often, until almost
boiling. Remove from heat; stir in sour cream. To serve, spoon beef
mixture onto tortillas; add desired garnishes and roll up. Spoon cheese
sauce over burritos. Makes 6 to 8 servings.

A paste made of equal parts
cream of tartar and vinegar is
a great mixture for removing
stains on a slow cooker.
Just rub on, then rinse well.

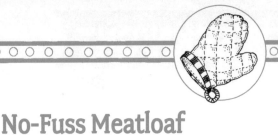

No-Fuss Meatloaf

Kathy DeSchinckel
Davenport, IA

This is a recipe from Julie, one of the great cooks at our church.

1 lb. ground beef
1 lb. ground pork sausage
8-oz. container French onion dip

2 eggs, beaten
1 sleeve saltine crackers,
  crushed

In a large bowl, mix all ingredients together with your hands. Form into a loaf; place in a slow cooker. Cover and cook for 8 hours on low setting, or 4 hours on high setting, until no longer pink in the center. Makes 6 to 8 servings.

Easy Baked Potatoes

Kathy Grashoff
Fort Wayne, IN

My son Joe has been making these for years for his family's Christmas Eve open house. Bowls of sour cream, shredded cheese, bacon bits and other toppings are set out for a help-yourself potato bar. You may add as many potatoes as will fill your slow cooker.

6 to 8 baking potatoes

Wrap each potato in aluminum foil. Stack wrapped potatoes in slow cooker; do not add any liquid. Cover and cook on low setting for 10 hours, or on high setting for 6 hours, until potatoes are fork-tender. Makes 6 to 8 servings.

Potlucks and
GET-TOGETHERS

Braised Beef

Jessica Kraus
Delaware, OH

Put this delicious recipe into your slow cooker in the morning and forget about it until dinnertime. The sauce is delicious spooned over polenta.

3-lb. beef rump roast
salt and pepper to taste
3 T. olive oil
2 28-oz. cans whole tomatoes
1/2 c. beef broth
3 T. tomato paste

1 yellow onion, diced
3 cloves garlic, minced
1 t. dried basil
1 t. dried oregano
2 bay leaves
cooked polenta or thin spaghetti

Season roast with salt and pepper; set aside. Heat olive oil in a large, deep skillet over medium heat. Add roast; brown on all sides. Remove roast to a greased slow cooker. Top with undrained tomatoes and remaining ingredients except polenta or spaghetti. Spoon some of the mixture over roast. Cover and cook on low setting for 7 to 8 hours, until roast is very tender. Remove roast to a plate and shred with 2 forks. Discard bay leaves. Return beef to mixture in slow cooker; stir. Cover and cook on low setting for 15 additional minutes. To serve, ladle beef mixture over cooked polenta or spaghetti. Makes 6 servings.

Polenta is a terrific side dish for saucy Italian dishes. Topped with marinara sauce and sautéed mushrooms, it can even serve as a meatless main dish. Look for tubes of polenta in the supermarket's refrigerated section... easy to slice, heat and serve.

Salisbury Steak Meatballs

Liz Lanza
Charles Town, WV

This recipe is a spin on traditional Salisbury steak. Making meatballs and serving them over noodles is a fun treat for my family... it's a favorite!

2 lbs. ground beef
1-oz. pkg. onion soup mix
1/2 c. Italian-flavored dry
   bread crumbs
1/4 c. milk
1/4 c. all-purpose flour

2 T. oil
2 10-3/4 oz. cans cream of
   chicken soup
1-oz. pkg. au jus mix
3/4 c. water
cooked rice or egg noodles

In a large bowl, mix together beef, soup mix, bread crumbs and milk with your hands. Shape into golfball-size meatballs. Lightly coat meatballs in flour and shake off any excess flour. Heat oil in a skillet over medium-high heat. Working in batches, add meatballs to skillet; brown on all sides. Remove meatballs to a slow cooker; set aside. In a large bowl, combine soup, au jus mix and water. Whisk until smooth; pour over meatballs. Cover and cook on low setting for 4 to 5 hours, or on high setting for 3 to 4 hours. Serve meatballs over cooked rice or noodles. Makes 4 to 6 servings.

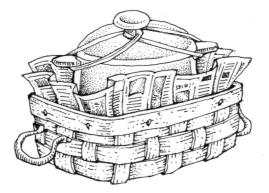

When toting a slow-cooker dish to a potluck, wrap a rubber band around one handle, bring it up over the lid and secure it over the other handle...the lid stays on nice and tight!

Cheesy Chicken Spaghetti

Tammy Sorensen
Sheffield, IA

When I made this recipe for the first time, my family loved it!
It makes enough to freeze half for another meal.

16-oz. pkg. spaghetti, uncooked
2 14-1/2 oz. cans petite diced
   tomatoes
16-oz. pkg. pasteurized process
   cheese, diced
2 c. boneless, skinless chicken
   breasts, cooked and chopped
3/4 c. water
4-oz. can mild green chiles

10-3/4 oz. can cream of
   mushroom soup
10-3/4 oz. can cream of chicken
   soup
4-oz. can mushroom stems and
   pieces, drained
1/2 c. onion, diced
salt and pepper to taste

Cook spaghetti according to package directions; drain. Spray a slow cooker with non-stick vegetable spray. Add cooked spaghetti to slow cooker. Top with undrained tomatoes and remaining ingredients; stir to mix well. Cover and cook on low setting for 3 to 4 hours, until bubbly and cheese is melted. Stir before serving. Makes 8 to 10 servings.

It's fine to fill a slow cooker with chilled ingredients, then set the crock's timer to start in one to 2 hours. If your slow cooker doesn't have a built-in timer, pick up an automatic timer at the hardware store and plug the crock right into it.

Fiesta Chicken Olé

Robin Muer
Encino, CA

This takes a little time but it is delicious. I like to slow-cook the chicken overnight, then prepare the recipe in the morning.

4 to 6 lbs. chicken pieces
1/2 c. water
10-3/4 oz. can cream of chicken soup
10-3/4 oz. can cream of mushroom soup

7-oz. can diced chiles
16-oz. pkg. shredded Cheddar cheese
16-oz. pkg. shredded Monterey Jack cheese
1 doz. corn tortillas, cut in strips

The night before, place chicken in a 6-quart slow cooker; add water. Cover and cook on low setting overnight, about 8 hours. In the morning, remove chicken to a large platter and cool slightly. Shred or cube chicken; discard bones and skin. Discard juices in slow cooker; wipe crock clean. Return shredded chicken to slow cooker; add remaining ingredients. Cover and cook on high setting for one to 2 hours, until bubbly and cheese is melted, stirring occasionally. Makes 8 servings.

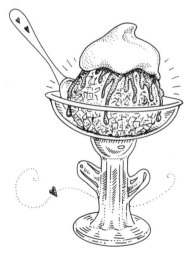

Serve up some "fried" ice cream with a Mexican feast. Freeze scoops of ice cream, roll in crushed frosted corn flake cereal and drizzle with honey. Top with cinnamon, whipped cream and a cherry. Yum!

Stuffed Cabbage Rolls

Ida Mannion
North Chelmsford, MA

This is a recipe my mom used to make for my dad. It was one of his favorite meals. My mom had eight children and this went a long way at mealtime. The vegetable juice is my own addition.

1 head cabbage, cored
3/4 c. quick-cooking rice,
  uncooked
1 egg, lightly beaten
1/2 c. onion, diced

salt to taste
1-1/2 lbs. lean ground beef
46-oz. can cocktail vegetable
  juice

Add cabbage to a large pot of boiling water. Cook just until cabbage leaves fall off head. Set aside 12 large leaves for rolls; drain well. In a large bowl, combine uncooked rice, egg, onion and salt. Crumble uncooked beef over mixture and mix well. Place 1/3 cup beef mixture on each cabbage leaf; overlap ends of leaf and fold in sides. Roll up completely to enclose filling; secure with wooden toothpicks, if desired. Place cabbage rolls in a slow cooker. Pour vegetable juice over rolls. Cover and cook on low setting for 6 to 7 hours. Makes 12 servings.

Fresh vegetables like potatoes, carrots and onions should be placed in the bottom and along the sides of a slow cooker, with the meat on top, as they generally take longer to cook.

All-Day Cassoulet

Beverlee Traxler
British Columbia, Canada

Twenty years ago, I started to use this hearty recipe when the kids and grandkids came to visit. My grandson Colbey is 22 years old now and still remembers, "Ah, Gramma's bean casserole." It is delicious and well-liked by all. Hope your family enjoys this as much as mine does!

1-1/2 lbs. smoked Polish
   sausage, sliced 1/4-inch
   thick
3 c. shredded Cheddar cheese
2 14-oz. cans kidney beans
2 14-oz. cans pork & beans
14-oz. can lima beans, drained
10-3/4 oz. can tomato soup

1 onion, chopped
1/2 c. green, red or yellow
   pepper, diced
1/4 c. golden syrup or dark
   corn syrup
1/2 t. dry mustard
1/2 t. pepper

Place all ingredients in a slow cooker; do not drain kidney beans or pork & beans. Stir gently. Cover and cook on low setting for 8 to 10 hours. This dish freezes well. Makes 10 servings.

A family recipe book is a wonderful way to preserve one generation's traditions for the next. Ask everyone to share their most-requested recipes, just the way they make them. Arrange handwritten or typed recipes into a book and have enough copies made for everyone. Sure to be cherished!

Yankee Pot Roast

Sharon Vuyanich
North Versailles, PA

A friend gave me this recipe and I've been using it for 20 years. It's foolproof! Very quick and simple. This recipe reminds me of when my mom used to make a Sunday dinner that took hours to prepare.

3 to 4-lb. beef chuck roast
garlic powder, salt and pepper
   to taste
1 to 2 T. oil
2 to 3 carrots, peeled and sliced
1 onion, cut into chunks
1 to 2 green, red and/or yellow
   peppers, cut into chunks

3 to 4 potatoes, peeled and
   cubed
14-1/2 oz. can diced tomatoes
12-oz. jar beef gravy
1/4 to 1/2 c. red wine or beef
   broth
1 bay leaf

Season roast with garlic powder, salt and pepper; set aside. Heat oil in a large skillet over medium heat. Add roast; brown well on all sides. Add carrots to a slow cooker. Top with roast, onion, peppers and potatoes; set aside. To a 4-cup measuring cup, add tomatoes with juice and gravy. Add enough wine or beef to make 4 cups of liquid. Pour mixture over roast; top with bay leaf. Cover and cook on high setting for 3 to 4 hours. Turn slow cooker to low setting; continue cooking for 3 to 4 hours, or until roast is fork-tender and vegetables are still firm. Discard bay leaf before serving. Makes 4 to 6 servings.

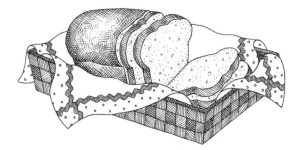

Whip up a loaf of beer bread for dinner. Combine 2 cups self-rising flour, a 12-ounce can of beer and 3 tablespoons sugar in a greased loaf pan. Bake for 25 minutes at 350 degrees, then drizzle with melted butter. Warm and tasty!

Pot Roast Dinner

Beverley Williams
San Antonio, TX

This is one of my family's favorite dinners. The slow cooker
makes it so easy for those busy days.

2 to 3-lb. beef chuck roast
1 t. garlic powder
3 c. beef broth, divided
2 russet potatoes, peeled and
    cubed

3 to 4 carrots, peeled and sliced
1 T. dried basil
1 t. dried oregano

Sprinkle roast evenly with garlic powder. Place in a slow cooker; add 2 cups broth. Cover and cook on high setting for 3-1/2 hours. Add potatoes, carrots, herbs and remaining broth to slow cooker. Cover and continue cooking on high setting for an additional hour, or until roast and vegetables are tender. Makes 6 to 8 servings.

Darn Good Cola-Chili Roast

Anna Rendell
Burnsville, MN

Good friends shared this recipe with us years ago, and it's our
favorite to serve on a chilly winter evening! My grandpa especially
loved the au jus that this recipe makes and would call it "soup,"
slurping it right from a bowl. Our busy family loves the simplicity of
this recipe. It makes a supremely tender and flavorful roast.

2-lb. beef chuck roast
1-oz. pkg. onion soup mix
12-oz. can cola

12-oz. bottle chili sauce
3 potatoes, peeled and cubed
3 carrots, peeled and sliced

Place roast in a slow cooker and sprinkle with soup mix. Pour cola and chili sauce over roast. Cover and cook on low setting for 6 hours. Add vegetables; cover and cook 2 more hours, or until roast and vegetables are tender. Makes 4 to 6 servings.

Cowboy Beans

Dana Rowan
Spokane, WA

A lady at our church used to make yummy homemade barbecue beans for church potlucks, but we moved away before I could get her recipe. I experimented and came up with these beans that we enjoy as a main course with cornbread. They are so good, and filling too.

1/2 lb. bacon, crisply cooked and crumbled
1/2 lb. ground beef
1/2 lb. ground pork breakfast sausage
1/2 c. onion, chopped
16-oz. can pork & beans
16-oz. can pinto or chili beans
16-oz. can butter beans, drained
16-oz. can kidney beans, drained

1/4 c. catsup
1/4 c. barbecue sauce
1/4 c. brown sugar, packed
1/4 c. molasses
2 T. mustard
1 T. chili powder
1 t. garlic salt
1 t. Montreal steak seasoning or pepper

In a skillet over medium heat, cook bacon until crisp; drain and crumble. In a separate skillet over medium heat, cook beef and sausage until browned. Add onion and cook until tender; drain well. Add bacon and beef mixture to a slow cooker. Add undrained pork & beans, undrained pinto or chili beans and remaining ingredients. Stir gently. Cover and cook on high setting for one hour. Reduce heat to low setting; cover and cook for an additional 2 to 4 hours. Taste and adjust seasonings as needed. Makes 8 to 10 servings.

A fun new way to serve cornbread...waffle-style! Mix up the batter, thin it slightly with a little extra milk and bake in a waffle iron until crisp. Terrific for dunking!

Black Beans & Sausage

Janis Parr
Ontario, Canada

This tasty dish is great for a group gathering or potluck.
You're sure to be asked for the recipe!

2 lbs. smoked pork sausage,
    cut into bite-size pieces
1-1/2 c. onion, chopped
3 cloves garlic, chopped
28-oz. can crushed tomatoes
3 15-oz. cans black beans,
    drained
1-1/2 c. celery, chopped

2 cubes chicken bouillon,
    crumbled
2 t. dried thyme
1-1/2 t. dried oregano
1 t. pepper
1/8 t. cayenne pepper
cooked rice

In a large skillet over medium heat, brown sausage, onion and garlic until sausage is cooked through. Drain; transfer sausage mixture to a large slow cooker. Add tomatoes with juice and remaining ingredients except rice; stir to combine. Cover and cook on low setting for 8 hours, or on high setting for 4 hours. Serve over a bed of cooked rice. Makes 8 to 10 servings

Keep bugs away from cool picnic beverages. Simply poke a hole through a paper cupcake liner, add a straw, flip it upside-down and use it as a beverage cap.

Scalloped Potatoes

Carolyn Gochenaur
Howe, IN

I have no idea where I got this recipe years ago, but my family likes it and it goes over well at potlucks. I like to cook it overnight. Feel free to mix & match the flavors of cream soup.

6 to 8 potatoes, peeled, thinly sliced and divided
salt and pepper to taste
Optional: 2 c. cooked ham, diced and divided

2 10-3/4 oz. cans cream of mushroom, celery and/or Cheddar cheese soup
12-oz. can evaporated milk

Spray a slow cooker with non-stick vegetable spray. Layer potatoes in slow cooker, adding salt and pepper to each layer, until slow cooker is 3/4 full. Add some ham to each layer, if using. In a bowl, whisk together soups and evaporated milk. Pour over potatoes; stir gently. Cover and cook on low setting for 8 hours, or until potatoes are very tender. Stir occasionally, if possible. Makes 10 to 12 servings.

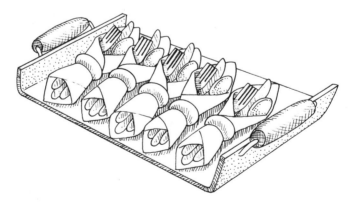

For a dinner party or holiday buffet, roll up sets of flatware in table napkins and place in a shallow tray. An easy do-ahead for the hostess...guests will find it simple to pull out individual sets too.

Creamy Potluck Corn

Ann Mathis
Biscoe, AR

This dish is always a hit at potluck suppers and picnics. It's so easy and I always have the ingredients on hand.

3 12-oz. pkgs. frozen corn
8-oz. pkg. cream cheese, cubed
1/4 c. butter, cubed

2 T. sugar
1 t. salt
1 t. pepper

Place corn in a slow cooker. Add remaining ingredients; stir well. Cover and cook on low setting for 4 hours, or on high setting for 2 hours. Stir at least once, halfway through cooking time. Makes 8 to 10 servings.

Make a table tent to announce what you've brought to the potluck. Glue a sweet fabric yo-yo or two to a folded card, write the recipe name on the card and set it beside the dish.

Seafood Ravioli

Missy Abbott
Hickory, PA

I came up with this recipe trying to convert my family's love of seafood lasagna into a quick & easy task. I achieved it with this delicious recipe! I use my 13"x9" casserole slow cooker for this, but a regular slow cooker can be used instead. Give it a try!

2 16-oz. jars Alfredo sauce, divided
24-oz. pkg. frozen cheese ravioli, divided
8-oz. pkg. shredded mozzarella cheese, divided
16-oz. pkg. cooked cocktail shrimp, thawed and tails removed
12-oz. can crabmeat, drained and flaked
1/2 c. onion, finely chopped
16-oz. pkg. frozen chopped spinach, thawed and squeezed dry
1 t. granulated or powdered garlic
1/2 t. salt
1/4 t. pepper

Spray a large slow cooker with non-stick vegetable spray. Spread 1/4 cup Alfredo sauce evenly in the bottom of slow cooker. Layer with half each of frozen ravioli and cheese; add half of remaining sauce. Layer all of shrimp, crabmeat, onion and spinach, adding seasonings between layers as desired. Top with remaining ravioli and remaining sauce. Cover and cook on low setting for 6 to 8 hours. About 30 minutes before serving, sprinkle remaining cheese on top. Cover and cook on low setting another 30 minutes, or until cheese melts. Makes 6 servings.

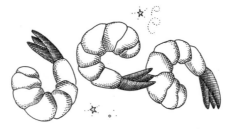

Keep frozen shrimp on hand for delicious meals anytime.
Thaw it quickly by placing the shrimp in a colander and
running cold water over it...ready to use!

GET-TOGETHERS

3-Cheese Spinach Lasagna
JoAnn

Perfect for a busy day with company coming for dinner.
Not having to precook the lasagna noodles is a bonus.

2 15-oz. containers ricotta
   cheese
8-oz. pkg. shredded mozzarella
   cheese, divided
1/2 c. grated Parmesan cheese,
   divided
10-oz. pkg. frozen chopped
   spinach, thawed and
   squeezed dry

2 eggs, beaten
1-oz. pkg. vegetable soup mix
2 24-oz. jars favorite pasta
   sauce, divided
12 lasagna noodles, uncooked
   and divided

In a large bowl, combine ricotta cheese, one cup mozzarella cheese, 1/4 cup Parmesan cheese, spinach, eggs and soup mix. Stir well and set aside. Spread one cup pasta sauce in a large slow cooker. Layer with 4 lasagna noodles, broken to fit; add one cup pasta sauce and half of ricotta mixture. Repeat; top with remaining lasagna noodles and 2 cups pasta sauce. Reserve remaining cheeses and pasta sauce in the refrigerator. Cover and cook on low setting for 5 to 6 hours. Sprinkle with remaining cheeses; cover and cook on low setting an additional 10 minutes. Let stand 10 minutes before serving; cut into wedges. Heat remaining pasta sauce; ladle over portions of lasagna. Makes 8 servings.

Salad smarts! The darker the greens, the healthier they are for you. Try spinach or romaine lettuce...if iceberg lettuce is more to your liking, try a mix of iceberg and darker greens.

Italian Sausage, Pepper & Onion Crock

Myrna Barager
Ontario, Canada

A tasty dish that's great for tailgating get-togethers and potluck suppers. Add a big basket of warm crusty bread.

2-1/2 lbs. sweet or hot Italian
  pork sausage links
1-1/2 yellow onions, halved,
  cut into 1/2-inch slices and
  divided
2 green peppers, cut into 2-inch
  squares and divided
1 red pepper, cut into 2-inch
  squares and divided
4 cloves garlic, chopped
2 T. fresh basil, chopped

4 bay leaves
28-oz. can whole tomatoes,
  chopped, drained and juice
  reserved
6-oz. can tomato paste
1/2 c. dry red wine or beef broth
2 T. fresh parsley, chopped
1 T. dried oregano
1/2 t. salt
1/4 t. pepper

Cut each sausage into 2 pieces. Brown sausages in a large skillet over medium-high heat; drain and set aside. In a large slow cooker, layer half each of onions and peppers. Add all sausages, remaining onions and peppers, garlic, basil, bay leaves and tomatoes. In a bowl, mix reserved tomato juice, tomato paste and wine or broth; pour over all. Cover and cook on low setting for 6 hours, or on high setting for 3 hours. At the beginning of final hour, mix remaining ingredients; add to slow cooker. Cover and cook one more hour, or until sausages are done and peppers are tender. Discard bay leaves before serving. Makes 8 servings.

Going tailgating? Pack a handyman-style toolbox with all the things that often get forgotten...grill tongs, a can opener, salt and pepper, you name it. You'll be a winner every time!

Fake-Out Italian Briciole

Andrea Vernon
Logansport, IN

This is my version of an Italian rolled steak dish. It is so easy to put everything in the crock and come home to a fabulous meal! I got the recipe from a friend and have played around with it until I came up with this version. Don't leave out the raisins...they're what makes this special. It's a very Italian thing!

3 to 4-lb. beef chuck roast
salt and pepper to taste
1 T. olive oil
2 cloves garlic, chopped
1/2 c. red wine or beef broth
24-oz. jar pasta sauce, or 3 c.
   homemade pasta sauce
1/2 c. grated Parmesan cheese

4-oz. can sliced mushrooms,
   drained
1/4 c. raisins
cooked rigatoni pasta or other
   hearty pasta
Garnish: additional grated
   Parmesan cheese

Season roast with salt and pepper; set aside. Heat oil in a heavy skillet over medium heat. Add roast and brown on each side for 3 minutes. Remove roast to a slow cooker. To drippings in skillet, add garlic and cook for 2 minutes; add wine or broth and scrape up the browned bits. Bring to a boil; pour skillet mixture over roast. In a bowl, mix together pasta sauce, cheese, mushrooms and raisins; pour over roast. Cover and cook on low setting for 6 to 8 hours, until roast is very tender. Serve with cooked pasta, garnished with additional Parmesan cheese. Makes 4 to 6 servings.

Broiled roma tomatoes make a tasty, quick garnish. Place tomato halves cut-side up on a broiler pan. Toss together equal amounts of Italian-seasoned dry bread crumbs and grated Parmesan cheese with a little oil. Spoon onto tomatoes and broil until golden.

All-in-the-Pot Jambalaya

Wendy Ball
Battle Creek, MI

I've had this recipe for quite awhile. My husband Dave used to volunteer for our town's Balloon Festival. Some of our friends working at the festival, military guardsmen, police officers and sheriffs, were all getting pretty tired of eating fair food. So, one day I decided to make enough jambalaya to feed a crowd. It was a huge success. Some of the guardsmen said it was even better than their commander's jambalaya. Now, that was a compliment! From then on, until we stopped volunteering, they always requested I bring in a BIG batch of this jambalaya for them...I sure did!

1 T. olive oil
1 T. butter
1 lb. boneless, skinless chicken
    or turkey breast, cubed
1 onion, diced
2 stalks celery, diced
1 green, red or yellow pepper,
    chopped
1 lb. pkg. spicy or mild smoked
    beef or turkey sausage,
    sliced
1 t. ground cumin
1 t. chili powder

1 t. poultry seasoning
pepper to taste
1 to 2 bay leaves
1 t. Worcestershire sauce
Optional: 5 drops hot pepper
    sauce
14-oz. can chicken broth
14-1/2 oz. can diced tomatoes
1 lb. medium shrimp, cleaned,
    cooked and peeled
2 c. cooked rice
Garnish: chopped green onions

Heat oil and butter in a skillet over medium-high heat. Add chicken or turkey; cook for 3 to 5 minutes per side, until golden but not cooked through. In a large slow cooker, layer chicken or turkey, vegetables and sausage. Add seasonings and sauces; top with broth and undrained tomatoes. Cover and cook on low setting for 6 to 8 hours, or on high setting for 4 to 6 hours. About 30 minutes before serving, add shrimp and cooked rice; mix gently. If mixture appears too dry, add additional broth or juice. Discard bay leaves; garnish servings with green onions. Makes 8 to 10 servings.

Corn & Sausage Bake

Debbie Densmore
Tunbridge, VT

My children love this dish and can't get enough of it. The recipe is great for family gatherings as it makes a lot, but it's easily halved for a smaller group. We have taken it to many get-togethers and are always asked for the recipe.

1 lb. smoked Polish sausage,
    diced
2 32-oz. pkgs. frozen corn,
    thawed
2 8-oz. pkgs. cream cheese,
    cubed
1/4 c. butter, cubed

3 T. milk
3 T. water
2 T. sugar
8-oz. pkg. shredded extra sharp
    Cheddar cheese
Optional: 1/2 c. onion, chopped

Brown sausage in a skillet over medium heat; drain. Place sausage in a 6-quart slow cooker; add remaining ingredients. Cover and cook on low setting for 4 hours, or on high setting for 2 hours, until heated through and cheeses are melted. Stir before serving. Makes 16 servings.

Frozen veggies are so handy in slow-cooker recipes.
Run cold water over them in a colander to
separate them easily.

Ropa Vieja

Jenessa Yauch
Munhall, PA

*This is an old Cuban recipe which literally translates
to "old clothes." It is very flavorful.*

1 T. oil
2-lb. beef flank steak or
    London broil
8-oz. can tomato sauce
6-oz. can tomato paste
1 c. beef broth
1/2 c. yellow onion, diced

1 green pepper, sliced into strips
1 T. vinegar
2 cloves garlic, minced
1 t. ground cumin
1 t. dried cilantro
cooked yellow or white rice

Heat oil in a skillet over medium heat; brown beef on both sides.
Drain; transfer to a slow cooker. Add remaining ingredients except rice;
stir. Cover and cook on low setting for 8 hours, or on high setting for
4 hours, until beef is tender. Shred beef in slow cooker; stir well and
serve over cooked rice. Makes 6 servings.

They say a person needs just three things to be truly happy
in this world: someone to love, something to do and
something to hope for.

– Tom Bodett

Caribbean Chicken & Veggies

Amy Bradsher
Roxboro, NC

I love to serve meals made from scratch, but they can be pretty time-consuming. This recipe is super-simple and cooks on its own, requiring little attention from me. Best of all, my kids love it!

1 lb. boneless, skinless
    chicken tenders
1 c. canned diced pineapple
    with juice
1 onion, coarsely chopped
1 green pepper, coarsely
    chopped

3/4 c. Caribbean-style marinade
2 c. canned black beans, drained
1 lb. broccoli, cut into bite-size
    flowerets
cooked rice

Combine chicken, pineapple with juice, onion, green pepper and marinade in a slow cooker. Cover and cook on low setting for 4 to 5 hours, until chicken is nearly cooked. Add black beans and broccoli. Cover and cook for another hour, or until broccoli is tender. Serve chicken mixture over cooked rice. Makes 4 to 6 servings.

Keep all those garden-fresh veggies fresh longer. Most veggies should be kept in the refrigerator with the exception of potatoes, sweet potatoes, onions and eggplant. Tomatoes will keep their flavor best if stored on the counter, not in the refrigerator.

Barbecued Beef Strips

Wendy Ball
Battle Creek, MI

I collect old recipes and look for them in the oddest places, Goodwill, Salvation Army, estate or book sales. Sometimes I find them on my doorstep. I have great neighbors who know I love to cook! This recipe is simple to fix, makes its own barbecue sauce and no special ingredients are needed. Perfect when you have a busy day ahead.

3 T. mustard
2-lb. beef top round steak, cut
   into 3-inch by 1-1/2 inch
   strips
1/2 c. onion, minced
1/2 c. green pepper, chopped
1/4 c. celery leaves, chopped
1/4 c. fresh parsley, minced
8-oz. can tomato sauce
1/4 c. cider vinegar

1-1/2 c. water
2 T. brown sugar, packed
2 T. all-purpose flour
1 t. garlic, minced
1/2 t. kosher salt
Optional: 1/4 t. cayenne pepper
cooked rice or noodles, or
   warmed buns and favorite
   sandwich toppings

Place mustard in a large bowl. Add beef and stir until well coated. Place beef in a slow cooker. In a separate bowl, combine remaining ingredients except rice, noodles or buns; stir well. Pour mixture over beef. Cover and cook on low setting for 6 to 8 hours, or until beef is tender. Serve beef mixture over cooked rice or noodles, or spoon onto buns and add desired toppings. Makes 5 to 6 servings.

Invite your friends and neighbors to a good old-fashioned block party. Set up picnic tables, arrange lots of chairs in the shade and invite everyone to bring a favorite slow-cooker dish. Whether it's a summer cookout or a fall harvest party, you'll make some wonderful memories together!

Lynn's Easy Beef Stroganoff

Lynn Lind
Deming, NM

I've had this recipe more than 30 years. The first time I served it, I had invited my parents to see my new apartment after moving out of their house. As they waited, I added the sour cream to the slow cooker...the final step...and gazed in amazement as it instantly curdled! I served it with an apology, and we ate it anyway, as it did taste good. My mother advised me on how to avoid that in the future.

1 onion, coarsely diced
1-1/2 to 2 lbs. stew beef cubes
1/2 lb. sliced mushrooms
1/2 t. garlic salt
salt and pepper to taste

1 c. water
Optional: 1/4 c. favorite red wine
8-oz. container sour cream
16-oz. pkg. wide egg noodles,
    cooked

Spray a slow cooker with non-stick vegetable spray. Add onion, beef and mushrooms; sprinkle with seasonings. Add water and wine, if desired. Cover and cook on high setting for 30 minutes to one hour, if possible. Turn slow cooker to low setting and cook for 8 hours, or until beef is very tender. At serving time, add a large spoonful of beef mixture to sour cream and stir. Repeat this step until all of beef mixture is incorporated. Serve over cooked noodles. Makes 4 to 6 servings.

The easiest-ever way to cook egg noodles...bring a big pot of water to a rolling boil, then add the noodles. Remove from heat, cover and let stand for 20 minutes, stirring twice. Perfect!

Janet's Meat Sauce

Janet Dolbow
West Deptford, NJ

My whole family loves my hearty slow-cooked meat sauce.

1 lb. mild ground pork sausage
1 lb. ground pork, beef and
   veal mix
1 onion, chopped
8 cloves garlic, finely chopped
28-oz. can diced tomatoes
29-oz. can tomato sauce

2 6-oz. cans tomato paste
2 T. dried basil
1 T. dried oregano
1 T. sugar
1 t. salt
1/2 t. pepper
cooked pasta

In a skillet over medium heat, combine sausage, meat mix, onion and garlic. Cook until browned, stirring occasionally, about 10 minutes. Drain. In a large slow cooker, combine tomatoes with juice and remaining ingredients except pasta; stir. Add meat mixture to sauce; stir well. Cover and cook on low setting for 9 hours, stirring occasionally. Serve sauce over cooked pasta. Makes 12 servings.

A whimsical centerpiece for an Italian dinner! Take a handful of long pasta like spaghetti, bucatini or curly strands of fusilli, and fan it out in a wide-mouthed vase.

Alice's Marinara Sauce

Alice Hardin
Antioch, CA

I created this meatless recipe as a healthier pasta sauce alternative. I love to serve it over cooked spaghetti squash instead of pasta...my family actually prefers it that way!

2 28-oz. cans crushed tomatoes
   with Italian herbs
6-oz. can tomato paste
1 onion, chopped
8 cloves garlic, finely chopped
1 T. olive oil
2 t. sugar

2 t. dried basil
1 t. dried oregano
1 t. salt
1 t. pepper
cooked spaghetti squash
   or pasta

In a 4-quart slow cooker, combine tomatoes with juice and remaining ingredients except pasta; stir. Cover and cook on low setting for 8 to 10 hours, or on high setting for 4 to 5 hours. Serve over cooked spaghetti squash or pasta. Makes about 6 cups, or 12 servings.

Keep a few packages of frozen cheese ravioli, tortellini or pierogies tucked in the freezer for easy meals anytime. Quickly cooked and topped with your favorite sauce, they're terrific as either a side dish or a meatless main.

Cheesy Scalloped Potatoes

Gladys Kielar
Whitehouse, OH

We love these delicious potatoes with their made-from-scratch Swiss cheese sauce and crumb topping.

6 c. potatoes, peeled and thinly
    sliced
4-oz. jar sliced pimentos,
    drained and chopped
1/4 c. onion, finely chopped
5 T. butter, divided
2 T. all-purpose flour

1/2 t. dry mustard
1/2 t. Worcestershire sauce
1/8 t. pepper
3 c. milk
1 c. shredded Swiss cheese
1-1/2 c. soft bread crumbs

Combine potatoes, pimentos and onion in a slow cooker; set aside. Melt 3 tablespoons butter in a saucepan over medium-low heat. Blend in flour, mustard, Worcestershire sauce and pepper. Stir in milk; cook and stir until thickened and bubbly. Add cheese; stir until melted. Stir cheese sauce into potato mixture; blend well. Cover and cook on low setting for 5-1/2 to 6-1/2 hours, or on high setting for 2-1/2 to 3-1/2 hours, until potatoes are tender. Melt remaining butter; toss with bread crumbs and sprinkle over potatoes. Cook, uncovered, for 30 minutes more. Makes 6 servings.

Make a quick condiment kit for your next picnic. Just place mustard, catsup, flatware and napkins in an empty cardboard soda pop carrier...so easy!

Old-Fashioned Baked Beans

Beverley Williams
San Antonio, TX

This was my grandmother's recipe. I grew up eating these beans in Tennessee. I usually do the first step overnight.

2 c. dried Great Northern beans,
   rinsed and sorted
5 c. water
1/2 c. onion, finely chopped
2 thick slices bacon, coarsely
   chopped

1-1/2 t. salt
2 T. brown sugar, packed
1/4 c. catsup
1 t. dry mustard
1/4 c. molasses

Place dried beans in a slow cooker. Add water, onion, bacon and salt. Cover and cook on high setting for 8 to 10 hours. Drain beans, reserving one cup of the liquid. Add remaining ingredients along with reserved liquid; mix well. Cover and cook on high setting for an additional one to 2 hours. Makes 8 to 10 servings.

Slow-cooker meals make reunion dinners so easy! While dinner cooks, enjoy a game of baseball, croquet, hide & seek or just sitting in the shade catching up with one another.

Tangy Pork Roast

Andrea Lehman
Chalfant, CA

*I like it saucy! But the sauce ingredients can be halved
if you don't want as much sauce.*

1 yellow onion, sliced
2 to 3-lb. boneless pork loin
   roast
2 c. hot water
1/2 c. sugar
6 T. red wine vinegar
1/4 c. soy sauce

2 T. catsup
1 t. salt
1 t. pepper
1/2 t. garlic powder or
   minced garlic
1/8 t. hot pepper sauce

Arrange onion slices evenly in the bottom of a slow cooker. Place roast
on top. In a separate bowl, mix remaining ingredients well; pour over
roast. Cover and cook on low setting for 6 to 8 hours, until roast is
tender. Makes 6 servings.

Slow-cook a pot of creamy beans to serve with pork. Rinse and drain
1/2 pound dried navy beans. Place them in a slow cooker and stir in
one chopped onion, one tablespoon of bacon drippings or butter and
5 cups boiling water. Cover and cook on high for 4 hours, stirring
occasionally. Season with salt after the beans are tender.

Roast Pork with Fruit

Sandra Monroe
Preston, MD

Perfect for dinner parties...set the slow cooker and enjoy your guests!

1 onion, sliced
2-lb. boneless pork loin roast
8-oz. pkg. mixed dried fruit
1/2 c. apple juice

1/2 t. salt
1/2 t. ground nutmeg
1/4 t. cinnamon

Place onion in a slow cooker that has been sprayed with non-stick vegetable spray. Add roast; top with fruit. Mix remaining ingredients in a cup and pour over fruit. Cover and cook on low setting for 7 to 9 hours, until pork is tender. Slice roast; serve with the fruit sauce from slow cooker. Makes 4 to 6 servings.

Hosting lots of guests for dinner? Feel free to mix & match plates and glasses for a whimsical look that's more fun than carefully matched china.

Chicken with White Wine & Cream

Judy Parks
Georgetown, TX

This is a favorite family dish that we often share at Christmas. Everyone likes it! We have a bay tree in our yard, so I just go out and pick the leaves to put in the recipe. Enjoy!

2 T. olive oil
3 lbs. boneless, skinless chicken thighs
3 boneless, skinless chicken breasts
1-1/4 lbs. sliced mushrooms
1 onion, coarsely chopped
1 t. salt
4 cloves garlic, minced
1-3/4 c. white wine

1 c. low-sodium chicken broth
1 t. dried thyme
2 bay leaves
1 lb. carrots, peeled and cut into 3-inch lengths
1 c. whipping cream
1/4 c. all-purpose flour
1 T. lemon juice
salt and pepper to taste

Heat oil in a large skillet over medium heat. Brown chicken on both sides. Remove chicken to a plate, reserving one tablespoon drippings in skillet. Add mushrooms, onion and salt to skillet. Cook over medium heat, stirring occasionally, for about 8 minutes. Stir in garlic; cook for 30 seconds. Stir in wine, scraping up any brown bits. Simmer until reduced by half, about 5 minutes. Pour mixture into a slow cooker. Shred chicken, if desired; add to slow cooker and stir to coat. Add broth and herbs; arrange carrots around the edge. Cover and cook on low setting for 4 hours. Transfer chicken to a large bowl; cover with aluminum foil. Reserve carrots and cooking liquid in slow cooker; discard bay leaves. Turn slow cooker to high setting. In a bowl, whisk together cream and flour until smooth; stir into mixture in slow cooker. Cover and cook until sauce is thickened, about 15 to 30 minutes. Stir in lemon juice; season with salt and pepper. Return chicken to slow cooker for 5 minutes. Serve chicken and carrots topped with sauce from slow cooker. Makes 6 servings.

Ruby Chicken

Ellie Brandel
Milwaukie, OR

For a speedy start in the morning, you can combine all the ingredients except the rice in a plastic zipping bag, then marinate overnight in the refrigerator.

2 lbs. boneless, skinless chicken breasts, cubed
1 onion, chopped
12-oz. can frozen orange juice concentrate, thawed
zest of 1 orange
1 orange, chopped

12-oz. pkg. fresh cranberries
1 c. sugar
2 T. oil
2 t. salt
1 t. pumpkin pie spice
cooked rice

Add all ingredients except rice to a slow cooker. Cover and cook on low setting for 6 to 8 hours, until chicken juices run clear. Serve chicken and sauce from slow cooker over cooked rice. Makes 8 servings.

Need a quick, tasty side? Stir sautéed diced mushrooms, onion, green pepper or celery into prepared wild rice mix for a homemade touch.

Best-Ever Pineapple & Brown Sugar Ham

Kristy Wells
Ocala, FL

This is the juiciest, most tender ham I have ever eaten. I like to make this for Sunday dinner because it can be started before church and is ready to eat when we return home. Serve with all your favorite side dishes and enjoy!

5 to 6-lb. fully cooked
   bone-in ham
20-oz. can pineapple tidbits,
   drained and juice reserved

1 c. brown sugar, packed
1/2 c. honey
1-1/2 t. garlic, minced
salt and pepper to taste

Place ham in a large slow cooker, trimming to fit if necessary. Set aside pineapple tidbits. Mix together remaining ingredients in a bowl, adding reserved pineapple juice a spoonful at a time to make a glaze. Spoon enough of glaze mixture over the ham to cover it; refrigerate remaining glaze. Add pineapple tidbits around and over the ham. Cover and cook on high setting for 20 minutes per pound, or about 2 hours. Ham may be basted with its juices as it cooks, if desired. During the last 20 minutes of cooking time, spoon reserved glaze over ham. Remove ham to a platter; let stand several minutes before slicing. Makes 10 to 12 servings.

Make it easy for guests to mingle and chat...set up food at several tables instead of one big party buffet. Place hot foods on one table, chilled foods at another, sweets at yet another.

Maple Ham

Donna Riley
Gainesville, FL

*This ham is so easy and delicious...it is the only ham
my daughter likes! And your oven is free to cook other dishes.*

1 onion, sliced
5 to 7-lb. fully-cooked
  bone-in ham

1/2 c. pure maple syrup

Place onion in a large slow cooker. Place ham cut-side down on top of
onion. Pour maple syrup over ham. Cover and cook on low setting for
4 to 6 hours, basting ham with juices once each hour. Turn ham on its
side after 3 hours. Remove ham to a platter; let stand several minutes
before slicing. Makes 10 to 12 servings.

Potato Goodness

Ann Mathis
Biscoe, AR

*I love to fill up my slow cooker with this potato dish on a cold day.
I usually double the recipe...it's that good!*

30-oz. pkg. frozen diced
  potatoes
2 14-oz. cans chicken broth
1/2 c. onion, chopped
1/3 t. pepper

8-oz. pkg. cream cheese, cubed
Garnish: sour cream, shredded
  Cheddar cheese, sliced green
  onions

Combine all ingredients except garnish in a slow cooker; stir gently.
Cover and cook on low setting for 5 hours, until hot and bubbly.
Garnish as desired. Makes 6 to 8 servings.

Hosting a dinner party? Stick to
simple tried & true recipes you
know will turn out well. You'll be
happy and so will your guests.

Slow-Cooked Turkey Breast

Deirdre Edgette
Lima, OH

I made this for my husband and myself one Thanksgiving and we loved it! We had lots of delicious leftovers for soup and sandwiches too. I also made it when we had our parish priest for dinner and he had seconds!

1-oz. pkg. onion soup mix	2 to 3 t. seasoned salt
2 T. garlic powder	5 to 6-lb. bone-in turkey breast
2 T. onion powder	1 to 2 T. butter, softened

In a small bowl, combine soup mix and seasonings; set aside. Pat turkey breast dry with paper towels. Trim off any excess skin, leaving the skin that covers the breast. Rub butter over the outside of breast and under the skin. Sprinkle generously with seasoning mixture; place some under the skin, if possible. Place in a large slow cooker that has been sprayed with non-stick vegetable spray. Cover and cook on high setting for one hour. Turn slow cooker to low setting and cook for 7 hours, or until juices run clear when thickest part of breast is pierced. Remove to a serving platter; let stand several minutes before slicing. Makes 10 to 12 servings.

Save time with double-duty recipes by reserving half for another meal. Use extra roast turkey as the start of a tasty noodle casserole, simmer shredded beef with barbecue sauce to serve in crusty buns...even spoon extra chili into taco salads. The only limit is your imagination.

Turkey Filling in a Crock

Gladys Brehm
Quakertown, PA

This is a tradition for us every Thanksgiving. It's a nice change from regular bread stuffing!

6 to 8 potatoes, peeled and
    quartered
3 T. butter, divided
1/4 to 1/2 c. milk
2 onions, chopped

2 to 3 stalks celery, chopped
1 loaf day-old bread, cubed
2 T. poultry seasoning
1/2 to 1 c. vegetable broth

Add potatoes to a large pot of boiling water. Cook over medium-high heat until tender; drain. Mash potatoes, adding 2 tablespoons butter and enough milk to moisten. Meanwhile, in a skillet over medium heat, sauté onions and celery in remaining butter for 2 to 3 minutes, until softened. Stir onion mixture into mashed potatoes. Add bread cubes, seasoning and enough broth to moisten. Spray a slow cooker with non-stick vegetable spray; spoon in filling. Cover and cook on high setting for 2 to 3 hours. Serves 10.

Make some cranberry-orange sauce. In a saucepan, combine one cup water and one cup sugar; bring to a boil. Stir in a 12-ounce bag of fresh cranberries, the zest of 2 oranges, and then the oranges, chopped. Return to a boil. Simmer over low heat for 10 minutes, stirring several times. Serve warm or chilled.

Easy Chicken & Noodles

Ramona Storm
Gardner, IL

This smells so good and warms you up on a cold day. Leftover cooked chicken works great. Add some warm, crusty bread and a citrus salad...dinner is served!

16-oz. pkg. frozen egg noodles, uncooked
2 14-1/2 oz. cans chicken broth
2 10-3/4 oz. cans cream of chicken soup
1/2 c. onion, finely chopped

1/2 c. carrot, peeled and diced
1/2 c. celery, diced
salt and pepper to taste
2 c. boneless, skinless chicken breasts, cooked and cubed

Thaw egg noodles (or run package under warm water) just enough to break apart; set aside. Spray a slow cooker with non-stick vegetable spray. Add remaining ingredients except chicken; blend well. Stir in noodles and chicken. Cover and cook on low setting for 7 to 8 hours, until hot and bubbly. Makes 8 servings.

An edible centerpiece is so easy! Simply pile colorful fruit in a basket, then tuck nuts into the spaces in between. Try lemons and almonds in the summer...apples and walnuts in the fall.

Chicken Pot Pie Stew

Joyceann Dreibelbis
Wooster, OH

This comfort food will remind you of chicken pot pie...but there's no need to make a crust. I like to bake crescent roll dough flat on a baking sheet to form toppers.

4 boneless, skinless chicken
   thighs or breasts, cubed
10-3/4 oz. can cream of chicken
   soup
1 c. chicken broth
5 redskin potatoes, cubed
1 c. carrots, peeled and chopped
1 c. celery, chopped

1/4 c. onion, chopped
1 t. garlic, minced
1 t. celery seed
1 t. pepper
16-oz. pkg. frozen mixed
   vegetables
Optional: refrigerated crescent
   rolls or biscuits, baked

In a large slow cooker, combine all ingredients except frozen vegetables and rolls or biscuits. Cover and cook on low setting for 4 to 5 hours. Stir in frozen vegetables; cover and cook on low setting for one additional hour. If desired, serve over baked crescent rolls or split biscuits. Makes 12 to 15 servings.

kitchen
journal

Once you've planned a scrumptious menu for family & friends, be sure to take notes...you're likely to want to repeat it sometime down the road.

Pork Chops with Mushrooms

*Kavy Dover
Rochester, NH*

*A family favorite! This recipe is also delicious made
with four chicken breasts.*

4 to 6 pork loin chops,
   3/4-inch thick
1 T. oil
1/2 c. onion, thinly sliced
10-3/4 oz. can cream of
   mushroom soup
4-oz. can sliced mushrooms,
   drained
3/4 c. dry white wine or
   chicken broth

2 T. quick-cooking tapioca,
   uncooked
2 t. Worcestershire sauce
1 t. beef bouillon granules
3/4 t. dried thyme
1/4 t. garlic powder
cooked rice

In a skillet over medium heat, brown pork chops in oil on both sides; drain. Place onion in a 5-quart slow cooker; top with pork chops. In a bowl, combine remaining ingredients except rice; stir well and spoon over pork chops. Cover and cook on low setting for 8 hours. Serve pork chops and sauce from slow cooker over cooked rice. Makes 4 to 6 servings.

Keep side dishes simple. Boil new potatoes just until tender, then gently toss with butter and parsley. Quick & easy!

Colette's Sauerbraten

Pamela McCourt
Marlboro, NY

I received this recipe at least 35 years ago from my Aunt Colette, who was a good cook. It has become my favorite go-to for Christmas dinner. It is put together a few days ahead of time, then added to the crock Christmas morning. So easy and delicious!

3-1/2 to 4-lb. beef rump roast
1 c. cider vinegar
1 c. water
1 onion, sliced
1 lemon, sliced
2 T. sugar

2 T. salt
10 whole cloves
4 bay leaves
1/2 to 1 t. ground ginger
pepper to taste

Place roast in a large non-metallic bowl; set aside. In a small bowl, combine remaining ingredients except optional ingredients; mix well and pour over roast. Cover and refrigerate for 24 to 36 hours to marinate; turn several times. Place roast and marinade in a slow cooker. Cover and cook on low setting for 8 to 10 hours, or on high setting for 4 to 5 hours. Discard bay leaves before serving. Slice roast; serve with Gingersnap Gravy, if desired. Makes 8 servings.

Gingersnap Gravy:

cooking liquid from slow cooker, strained

10 gingersnap cookies, crumbled

Pour cooking liquid into a saucepan over medium heat; bring to a simmer. Stir in gingersnaps. Cook, stirring occasionally, until thickened, about 10 minutes.

One Hot Mamma Chicken

Lillian Child
Omaha, NE

I've discovered chipotles in adobo sauce and now use them in so many recipes. They have this fabulous smoky flavor that creates quite a kick of heat! Coming home to a house filled with luscious aromas makes me feel like I have a private cook...I can dream!

1-1/2 lbs. boneless, skinless
    chicken tenders
15-1/2 oz. can fire-roasted diced
    tomatoes, drained
1 to 2 chipotles in adobo sauce
1/4 c. tomato paste

1 onion, chopped
1 green pepper, chopped
1/2 t. vinegar
tortillas and taco toppings, or
    cooked Mexican rice

In a slow cooker, combine all ingredients except tortillas and toppings or rice. Cover and cook on low setting for 7 to 8 hours, or on high setting for 5 to 6 hours. Serve in tortillas with favorite toppings, or ladle over cooked rice. Serves 6 to 8.

Kate's Southwestern Chicken

Elaine Divis
Sioux City, IA

When my daughter Kate put together a "Welcome to our family" cookbook for her new sister-in-law, she included this recipe. It is a huge favorite!

2 15-1/2 oz. cans black beans,
    drained and rinsed
16-oz. jar chunky salsa
1 c. frozen corn
4 to 5 boneless, skinless chicken
    breasts

flour or corn tortillas
Garnish: shredded lettuce,
    chopped tomatoes, black
    olives, shredded cheese,
    sour cream

Combine beans, salsa and corn; add most of mixture to a slow cooker. Add chicken; pour remaining bean mixture on top. Cover and cook on low setting for 7 to 8 hours, until chicken is very tender. Shred chicken. Serve in tortillas, garnished as desired. Serves 6 to 10.

Chalupa Pot Roast

Carrie Sullivan
Eufaula, OK

This is always a crowd-pleaser for young and old alike! Delicious with very little effort, but be sure to start the night before. It's delicious with pork roast as well.

3-lb. beef chuck roast
1-oz. pkg. low-sodium taco
   seasoning mix
Optional: 1 c. water
10-oz. can diced tomatoes and
   green chiles
4-oz. can diced green chiles

14-oz. can black beans, drained
   and rinsed
flour or corn tortillas
Garnish: shredded Cheddar
   cheese, sour cream,
   guacamole

The night before serving, spray a slow cooker with non-stick vegetable spray. Place roast in slow cooker; sprinkle with seasoning mix. If a leaner cut of roast is used, add water. Cover and cook on low setting for 8 hours to overnight. Using 2 forks, shred beef in slow cooker. Add tomatoes with juice, chiles and beans. Cover and cook an additional 8 hours on low setting. Serve beef mixture on tortillas with desired toppings. Makes 8 servings.

Feeding a crowd? Serve festive Mexican or Italian dishes that everybody loves. They often feature rice or pasta, so they're filling yet easy on the pocketbook. The theme makes it a snap to put together the menu and table decorations too.

Dale's Pot Roast

Paula Benson
Caney, KS

I met my friend Dale when he was on-site doing long-term contract work. My group liked to cook meals often at work and we always invited our contractors to join us. When I found out Dale's favorite food was pot roast, I started making this especially for him.

1 lb. potatoes, quartered
2 c. baby carrots
2 red onions, coarsely chopped
4 stalks celery, cut into 2-inch
    pieces
2 parsnips, peeled and cut into
    2-inch pieces
2-1/2 lb. beef chuck roast, fat
    trimmed

3/4 c. beef broth
1/2 t. dried thyme
1 t. dried rosemary
1 bay leaf
1/4 c. all-purpose flour
1/2 c. cold water

Add vegetables to a slow cooker. Cut roast into serving-size pieces, if desired; add to slow cooker. Pour broth over roast. Sprinkle with seasonings; add bay leaf. Cover and cook on low setting for 8 to 10 hours, until roast is very tender. Remove roast and vegetables to serving dishes; cover. Discard bay leaf. If gravy is desired, measure out slightly over 2 cups of cooking liquid into a small saucepan. Additional broth may be added to equal 2 cups, if needed. Let stand several minutes; skim off fat. Bring to a boil over medium heat. Mix flour with cold water in a covered jar; shake until smooth. Whisk flour mixture into boiling liquid. Cook, stirring constantly, for one minute, or until thickened. Makes 6 to 8 servings.

For dark, rich-looking gravy, add a spoonful or two of brewed black coffee. It will add color to pale gravy but won't affect the flavor.

Italian Pot Roast

Catherine Butler
Spring Lake, MI

This pot roast has always been a family favorite on a cold winter's night. I remember when my grandma made it... the kitchen smelled so good.

1/2 lb. sliced baby portabella
    mushrooms
1 onion, halved and sliced
2-1/2 to 3-lb. beef chuck roast,
    trimmed
1-1/2 oz. pkg. garlic and herb
    sauce mix

1/2 t. red pepper flakes
2 14-1/2 oz. cans Italian-style
    diced tomatoes, drained
8-oz. can tomato sauce
2 T. cornstarch
2 T. cold water

Place mushrooms and onion in a 6-quart slow cooker; add roast. Sprinkle roast evenly with sauce mix and red pepper flakes. Pour tomatoes with juice and tomato sauce over roast. Cover and cook on high setting for 5 to 6 hours, until roast is very tender. Remove roast to a platter; cut into large chunks. Keep warm. For gravy, skim fat from cooking liquid in slow cooker; discard fat. Stir together cornstarch and cold water in a small bowl until smooth; add to juices in slow cooker, stirring until blended. Cover and cook on high setting for 20 to 30 minutes more, until mixture is thickened, stirring once. Add chunks of roast back to slow cooker. Cover and cook for a few minutes, until heated through. Makes 6 servings.

At Sunday dinner, bring the family together and share your blessings. Make it extra special with Mom's best lace tablecloth, Grandmother's sparkling silverware and fresh flowers in a vase... memories in the making!

Lemon-Rosemary Roast Chicken
Courtney Stultz
Columbus, KS

The slow cooker is one of my best friends. It makes roasting chicken a breeze! This chicken is great for spring gatherings as it features the light, fresh flavors of lemon and rosemary.

1 onion, diced
1 apple, peeled, cored and sliced
2 stalks celery, diced
3 to 4-lb. roasting chicken
1 T. olive oil
1 t. garlic, minced

1 T. fresh rosemary, chopped,
 or 1 t. dried rosemary
1 t. dried thyme
2 t. sea salt
1 t. pepper
1 lemon, sliced

Combine onion, apple and celery in a bowl. Remove giblets from chicken, if necessary. Stuff chicken with as much of onion mixture as possible. Add any remaining onion mixture to a large slow cooker. Place chicken in slow cooker; drizzle with oil. Combine garlic and seasonings in a cup; rub chicken with mixture. Arrange lemon slices over chicken. Cover and cook on high setting for about 4 hours (recommended for the juiciest chicken), or on low setting for 8 hours. Remove chicken to a serving platter; discard vegetables and fruit. Let stand several minutes before slicing. Makes 8 servings.

For crisp, golden skin, transfer your slow-cooked chicken to a rimmed baking dish when cooking time is complete. Bake at 500 degrees for 15 minutes. It's OK if your chicken is so moist and tender it falls apart into pieces...it will still be delicious!

GET-TOGETHERS

Chicken & Sausage Paella

Darrell Lawrey
Kissimmee, FL

Your friends will think you really worked hard on
this wonderful dish...we won't tell them otherwise!

2-1/2 to 3 lbs. boneless, skinless
   chicken thighs, cubed
1 T. oil
1/2 lb. smoked turkey sausage
   links, cut into chunks
1 onion, sliced
3 cloves garlic, minced
2 t. dried thyme
1/2 t. pepper

1/8 t. dried saffron or turmeric
14-1/2 oz. can chicken broth
1/2 c. water
14-1/2 oz. can diced tomatoes,
   drained
2 yellow and/or green peppers,
   thinly sliced
1 c. frozen green peas, thawed
cooked yellow or white rice

In a large skillet over medium heat, cook chicken in oil until golden on
all sides; drain. Place chicken in a large slow cooker; add sausage and
onion. Sprinkle with garlic and seasonings. Pour broth and water over
all. Cover and cook on low setting for 7 to 8 hours, or on high setting
for 3-1/2 to 4 hours. About 15 to 20 minutes before serving, stir in
tomatoes, peppers and peas. Cover and cook on low setting until
vegetables are tender. Serve mixture ladled over cooked rice. Makes
6 servings.

Try this flavorful salad alongside a rich-tasting main dish. Toss
together mixed greens, cherry tomatoes and thinly sliced red onion
in a salad bowl. Whisk together 1/4 cup each of balsamic vinegar
and olive oil, then drizzle over salad.

Slow-Cooker Lasagna

Lois Pryor
Farmerville, LA

*My daughter-in-law has made this lasagna several times
for us. It's delicious and no-fuss!*

1 lb. Italian ground pork
  sausage
1/2 c. onion, chopped
3 15-oz. cans Italian-style
  tomato sauce
2 t. dried basil
1/2 t. salt

8-oz. pkg. shredded mozzarella
  cheese, divided
15-oz. container ricotta cheese
1 c. grated Parmesan cheese
15 lasagna noodles, uncooked
  and divided

Cook sausage and onion in a skillet over medium heat for 6 to
8 minutes, stirring occasionally, until sausage is no longer pink;
drain. Stir in tomato sauce, basil and salt; set aside. In a bowl, combine
one cup mozzarella cheese with ricotta and Parmesan cheeses. Chill
remaining mozzarella cheese while lasagna cooks. Spoon 1/4 of
sausage mixture into a 6-quart slow cooker; top with 5 noodles, broken
into pieces to fit. Spread with half of cheese mixture and 1/4 of sausage
mixture. Top with 5 noodles, remaining cheese mixture and 1/4 of
sausage mixture. Top with remaining noodles and remaining sausage
mixture. Cover and cook on low setting for 4 to 6 hours, until noodles
are tender. Sprinkle remaining mozzarella cheese over top. Cover and
let stand for 10 minutes, or until cheese is melted. Makes 8 servings.

Tie rolled cloth napkins with ribbon and slip a fresh sprig
of sweet-scented thyme under the ribbon...charming!

Party Food

SNACKS AND SWEETS

BBQ Meatballs with a Kick

Beckie Apple
Grannis, AR

*Even if you're in a hurry, you can toss this together in minutes
and it will be waiting when you come home! It's a flavorful dinner
or party snack that's sure to be popular.*

32-oz. pkg. frozen homestyle
    meatballs
18-oz. bottle hot and spicy
    barbecue sauce
12-oz. bottle chili sauce

3 T. spicy brown mustard with
    horseradish
12-oz. jar grape, blackberry or
    apple jelly

Spray a slow cooker with non-stick vegetable spray; add meatballs and
set aside. In a large bowl, combine sauces and mustard; mix well and
spoon over meatballs. Spoon jelly over top. Cover and cook on low
setting for 4 to 6 hours, or on high setting for 3 to 4 hours. Makes
8 servings.

Invite friends over for snacks on game day. With hearty
appetizers simmering in a slow cooker or two, you'll be able
to relax and enjoy the big game with your guests.

Cranberry Chicken Wings

Courtney Stultz
Columbus, KS

We love chicken wings for appetizers! During the holidays we like this version. It features fruity holiday flavors with a little spice from chipotle and chili powders.

1 c. fresh cranberries
1 apple, peeled, cored and
    chopped
zest and juice of 1 orange
1/2 c. water
1/4 c. honey
1 T. soy sauce
1 t. garlic, minced

1 t. cinnamon
1 t. pepper
1/4 c. cornstarch
1 t. chili powder
1/2 t. chipotle powder
1 t. sea salt
4 lbs. chicken wings,
    cut into sections

In a saucepan, combine cranberries, apple, orange zest and juice, water, honey, soy sauce, garlic, cinnamon and pepper. Bring to a boil over medium heat; simmer for about 10 minutes, or until fruit is soft. In a large bowl, mix together cornstarch, spice powders and salt. Add chicken wings; toss to coat. Place wings in a large slow cooker. Spoon fruit sauce mixture over wings; toss to coat. Cover and cook on high setting for about 4 hours, until chicken juices run clear when pierced. Remove wings to a baking sheet. Bake, uncovered, at 400 degrees for about 10 minutes, until sauce is caramelized and golden. Makes 12 servings.

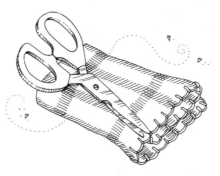

Section a big stack of chicken wings in a jiffy with sturdy kitchen shears. Afterwards, be sure to wash the shears with plenty of soapy water.

South-of-the-Border Dip

Darcy Geiger
Columbia City, IN

I make this dip for get-togethers...it's very easy and yummy!

2 lbs. ground pork sausage,
    browned and drained
3 14-1/2 oz. cans diced
    tomatoes with green chiles
1 c. favorite salsa
2 c. canned black beans, drained

2 c. canned corn, drained
32-oz. pkg. sharp Cheddar or
    queso blanco pasteurized
    process cheese, cubed
8-oz. pkg. cream cheese, cubed
tortilla chips

Combine sausage, tomatoes with juice and remaining ingredients except tortilla chips in a slow cooker; mix gently. Cover and cook on low setting for about 4 hours, until cheeses are melted. Stir before serving. Serve warm with tortilla chips. Makes 8 to 10 servings.

Why not try a light substitution? Low-fat cream cheese or Neufchâtel cheese have all the flavor but less fat than regular cream cheese.

Nacho Cheese Dip

Roberta Shay
Lawrenceburg, TN

I first tasted this dip at work years ago and loved it! Since then, it is a frequent request by friends and co-workers. It's also delicious spooned over a baked potato. Leftovers may be frozen, or so I have been told. I don't know, since I never have any leftovers!

1 lb. ground beef chuck, browned and drained
1 lb. hot pork breakfast sausage, browned and drained
32-oz. pkg. pasteurized process cheese spread, cubed

2 10-oz. cans diced tomatoes with green chiles, drained
10-3/4 oz. can cream of mushroom soup
tortilla chips

Combine all ingredients except tortilla chips in a slow cooker. Cover and cook on high setting for 3 hours, or until cheese is melted, stirring occasionally. Serve warm over tortilla chips. Makes 20 servings.

Shopping for a new slow cooker? Look for one that has a "warm" setting...it's perfect for keeping dips toasty through parties and potlucks.

Cranberry Meatballs

Tina Hengen
Clarkston, WA

I make these tasty meatballs whenever my son comes home and they are a must on our holiday table. You can use this same sauce to pour over little cocktail sausages as well.

5 doz. frozen meatballs
2 14-oz. cans jellied cranberry
　sauce
2 12-oz. bottles chili sauce
1/4 c. brown sugar, packed

3 T. Worcestershire sauce
2 T. mustard
1 T. molasses
garlic powder, salt and pepper
　to taste

Place meatballs in a slow cooker; set aside. Combine remaining ingredients in a saucepan; whisk over medium-high heat until smooth and hot. Pour over meatballs. Cover and cook on low setting for 3 to 4 hours, until sauce is bubbly and meatballs are heated through. Keep on low setting until ready to serve. Makes 5 dozen.

For an elegant yet easy last-minute party appetizer, drain a jar of Italian antipasto mix and toss with bite-size cubes of mozzarella cheese. Serve with cocktail picks.

Kielbasa Cocktail Appetizer

Thomas Campbell
Eden Prairie, MN

This recipe is one of my wife's favorites. She's not fond of Kielbasa, mustard or onions, but she likes this!

3 lbs. Kielbasa pork sausages, cut into 1-inch pieces
12-oz. jar apple jam

8-oz. jar mustard
2 T. dried, minced onion

Combine all ingredients in a slow cooker; stir gently. Cover and cook on high setting for 3 to 4 hours, stirring occasionally. Keep warm; serve with toothpicks. Makes 10 to 15 servings.

Sweet-and-Sour Kielbasa

Deborah Desrocher
Methuen, MA

Everyone loves this recipe...it serves so many and is so very simple to make. Enjoy!

3 to 4 14-oz. pkgs. Kielbasa sausage, cut into bite-size pieces

18-oz. bottle barbecue sauce
12-oz. jar currant or grape jelly

Combine all ingredients in a slow cooker; mix gently. Cover and cook on low setting for 2 to 3 hours, stirring occasionally. Keep warm. Makes 10 to 15 servings.

Love is the greatest refreshment in life.
– Pablo Picasso

Hot Artichoke & Spinach Dip

Jessica Shrout
Cumberland, MD

I tasted this wonderful dip at a friend's house and was one of many who requested the recipe. It's great to share with the family or take to a party...perfect for last-minute invites as well. It's delicious with almost everything!

2 14-oz. cans artichoke hearts,
    drained and chopped
10-oz. pkg. frozen spinach,
    thawed and squeezed dry
8-oz. container sour cream
3/4 c. grated Parmesan cheese
3/4 c. milk
1/2 c. crumbled feta cheese

1/2 c. onion, diced
1/3 c. mayonnaise
1 T. red wine vinegar
2 cloves garlic, pressed
1/4 t. pepper
8-oz. pkg. cream cheese, cubed
bread slices, pita chips or
    cut-up vegetables

In a slow cooker, combine all ingredients except cream cheese and bread, chips or vegetables. Stir until well combined; top with cream cheese. Cover and cook on low setting for 2 hours. Stir until cream cheese is well combined. Turn slow cooker to high setting; cover and cook for an additional 15 minutes. Serve warm with bread slices, pita chips or vegetables. Makes 8 servings.

Cut slices of crunchy carrot, zucchini and radish into stars,
flowers and other fun shapes with mini cookie cutters...
kids will eat their veggies happily!

192

Hanky-Panky Twist Dip

Nikki Marshall
Williamstown, KY

As a child, I grew up with my grandparents, who ate lots of country cooking at every meal. At the time I had no appreciation for that kind of food...it's amazing how you grow to love the little things. I learned to cook because I was allowed to experiment in the kitchen. I was always wanting to change the recipes I found...still do! The "twist" in this Hanky Panky Dip is Goetta, a local specialty.

1 lb. ground beef round
1 lb. ground hot pork sausage
1/2 lb. Goetta pork sausage or
    ground mild pork sausage
1/2 lb. pasteurized process
    cheese, cubed

1 t. garlic powder
1 t. seasoned salt
1/2 c. milk
round buttery crackers

In a large skillet over medium-high heat, brown meats together; drain. Place meat mixture in a 3-quart slow cooker; add cheese, garlic powder and salt. Add enough milk for desired consistency. Cover and cook on low setting for 2 hours, or until heated through and cheese is melted, stirring occasionally. Serve warm with crackers. Makes 25 servings.

Make a bridal shower gift extra special! Fill up a slow cooker with seasoning mix packets, herbs & spices, even a mini cookbook. The new bride will appreciate your thoughtfulness.

Bacon Horseradish Dip

Carol Davis
Edmond, OK

A hearty, zesty dip that men especially like.

2 c. shredded fontina cheese
8-oz. pkg. cream cheese, cubed
1 c. half-and-half
1/2 c. onion, chopped
1 clove garlic, finely minced

8 slices bacon, crisply cooked
  and crumbled
2 T. horseradish sauce
snack crackers, cut-up
  vegetables

Blend cheeses, half-and-half, onion and garlic in a 1-1/2 quart slow cooker. Cover and cook on low setting for 2-1/2 to 3 hours, until hot and bubbly. Stir in bacon and horseradish. Cover and cook on high setting about 15 minutes, until heated through. Serve warm with crackers and vegetables. Makes 24 servings.

Hot Tomato Cocktail

Liz Plotnick-Snay
Gooseberry Patch

A zippy beverage just right for chilly nights at the football stadium.

46-oz. can cocktail vegetable
  juice
2 T. brown sugar, packed
2 T. lemon juice

1-1/2 t. prepared horseradish
1 t. Worcestershire sauce
1/4 t. hot pepper sauce
1 stalk celery, cut into 3 pieces

Combine all ingredients in a 3-quart slow cooker; stir. Cover and cook on low setting for 3 to 4 hours. Discard celery; serve hot. Makes 6 to 8 servings.

Freshen up a thermos for hot drinks by spooning in a heaping teaspoon of baking soda, then filling with boiling water. Cap, shake gently and rinse... ready to go!

Reuben Dip

Katie Majeske
Denver, PA

Everyone's favorite sandwich in the form of a dip! It's great for entertaining...a Christmas tradition at our house.

1/2 lb. deli corned beef, chopped
14-1/2 oz. can sauerkraut,
  well drained
1 c. mayonnaise

2 c. shredded Swiss cheese
2 c. shredded Cheddar cheese
party rye bread

Combine all ingredients except bread in a slow cooker; mix well. Cover and cook on high setting for one to 2 hours, stirring occasionally, until cheeses are melted. Stir again. Serve warm, spread on bread slices. Makes 5 cups.

Need to chill lots of cans of soda pop? Just add beverages to an ice-filled cooler along with enough water to cover them, plus a generous amount of salt. The salt will lower the temperature quickly, cooling the drinks, and you'll save valuable refrigerator space too.

Buffalo Chicken Sliders

Jessica Shrout
Cumberland, MD

I first tried these tasty sliders at a party and have added a little more buffalo sauce. The blue cheese & celery dressing is my own addition. The celery gives it a crunch which we like, but it can be left out. You'll want to double the recipe for game days and get-togethers!

1 lb. boneless, skinless chicken breasts	1 T. butter, melted
3 to 5 T. buffalo wing sauce	16-oz. bottle blue cheese salad dressing, divided
1-1/2 T. ranch salad dressing mix	1/4 to 1/2 c. diced celery
	6 slider-size sandwich rolls, split

Place chicken breasts in a slow cooker. Add sauce, dressing mix and butter; mix gently. Cover and cook on low setting for 5 to 6 hours, until chicken is tender. Shred chicken in slow cooker, using 2 forks. Cover and cook on low setting for 10 to 20 more minutes. Meanwhile, in a small bowl, combine one cup salad dressing and desired amount of celery. To serve, divide chicken mixture among roll bottoms; top with dressing mixture and roll tops. Serve remaining salad dressing on the side. Makes about 6 servings.

Arrange a variety of mini breads, rolls and buns on a tiered cake stand alongside a variety of hot sandwich fillings and toppings. Guests will enjoy making different mini sandwiches to sample.

Buffalo Wing Dip

Darlene Bantam
Oxford, NE

I whipped up this recipe one game day when my husband said he was hungry for buffalo wings.

1-1/2 c. cooked chicken, diced
2 8-oz. pkgs. cream cheese, cubed
8-oz. pkg. shredded Pepper Jack cheese

8-oz. container sour cream
1/2 c. hot buffalo wing sauce
3 T. ranch salad dressing mix
corn chips, snack crackers, celery sticks

Combine all ingredients except chips, crackers and celery in a greased slow cooker. Cover and cook on low setting for one to 2 hours, or until cheeses are melted. Stir. Serve warm with corn chips, crackers and celery. Keeps well up to 8 hours on warm setting. Makes 20 servings.

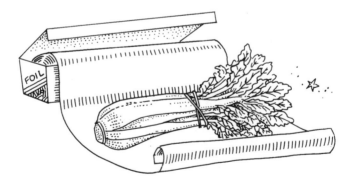

Keep celery crisp and green to the last stalk. Simply remove it from the plastic bag when you get home and keep the celery wrapped in aluminum foil.

Under-the-Sea Dip

Missy Abbott
Hickory, PA

I make this dip for all the seafood lovers who are tired of the same old dips being served at parties. Feel free to use your own favorite seafood.

10-3/4 oz. can cream of
  celery soup
10-3/4 oz. can cream of
  shrimp soup
2 c. cooked cocktail shrimp,
  cleaned and tails removed
6-oz. can crabmeat, drained
  and flaked

2 c. shredded Monterey Jack
  cheese
1/8 t. cayenne pepper
toast points or crusty Italian
  bread slices

Spray a 1-1/2 quart slow cooker with non-stick vegetable spray. Add all ingredients except toast points or bread slices; stir gently. Cover and cook on low setting for 2 to 3 hours. Serve warm with toast points or bread slices. Makes 8 to 10 servings.

Large scallop shells make clever serving containers for seafood dips. Use shells you've found on vacation, washed well, or check party supply stores for ready-to-use shells.

Jennie's Crab Dip

Jill Ball
Highland, UT

I first tasted this delicious dip at my friend Jennie's game-day party. I hovered over the bowl the whole time! She graciously shared her recipe with me and now it's a must-have whenever we're watching the big game.

3/4 c. mayonnaise
8-oz. pkg. cream cheese,
   softened
2 T. apple juice
1 onion, minced

1 lb. lump crabmeat, drained
   and flaked
pita chips, snack crackers,
   baguette slices or
   celery sticks

In a 3-quart slow cooker, mix mayonnaise, cream cheese and apple juice until blended. Stir in onion; mix well. Gently stir in crabmeat. Cover and cook on low setting for 4 hours, until hot and bubbly. Stir again. Serve with desired dippers. Makes 8 servings.

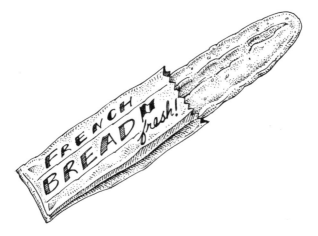

Creamy hot dips are twice as tasty with homemade baguette crisps. Thinly slice a French loaf and arrange slices on a baking sheet. Sprinkle with olive oil and garlic powder, then bake at 400 degrees for 12 to 15 minutes.

Steakside Mushrooms

Lisa Robason
Corpus Christi, TX

*A savory accompaniment to any steak dinner,
or serve with toothpicks for a delicious appetizer.*

2 lbs. small mushrooms,
   trimmed
2 c. dry red wine or beef broth
1/4 c. butter, sliced
1-1/2 t. Worcestershire sauce

2 cubes beef bouillon
1/2 t. garlic powder
1/2 t. onion powder
1/2 t. dried thyme
1/2 t. pepper

Combine all ingredients in a slow cooker; stir gently. Cover and cook
on high setting for 2 to 3 hours, until liquid is reduced by half. Makes
6 to 8 servings.

Planning an appetizers-only event? You'll want to serve
at least 5 different dishes...allow 2 to 3 servings
for each per person.

SNACKS ᴬⁿᴰ SWEETS

Zesty Cider-Cheddar Dip

Tiffany Brinkley
Broomfield, CO

My family just loves cheese! We're always trying new recipes for hot cheese dip and fondue, so when I found this recipe with an added zip of cider, we were pretty excited. We love it...you will too!

1 T. all-purpose flour
1 t. dry mustard
1/2 c. hard cider or apple cider
1 t. Worcestershire sauce
1 t. hot pepper sauce

2 c. shredded sharp Cheddar
   cheese
1/2 lb. pasteurized process
   cheese, cubed
pretzel rods, apple slices

Add flour and mustard to a 2-quart slow cooker; mix well and set aside. In a cup, combine cider and sauces; add to flour mixture and mix well. Stir in cheeses. Cover and cook on high setting for 1-1/2 hours, stirring twice, until cheese is melted and smooth. Serve warm with pretzels and apple slices. Makes 16 servings.

Come on Over

Remember that happy feeling you had as a kid when a party invitation arrived in the mail? Mail out written invitations to your next get-together, no matter how informal. Your grown-up friends will love it!

Festive Wassail

Nanette Hayles
Port Neches, TX

I make this warm punch every Thanksgiving and Christmas. I even make it for Halloween, to enjoy with popcorn as I watch my favorite scary movies! I like it either hot or cold. Whenever I've shared this recipe with family & friends, they want a copy of it too.

2 qts. apple cider
4 c. orange juice
2 c. pineapple juice
1 c. brown sugar, packed
4 3-inch cinnamon sticks

24 whole cloves
Optional: additional whole
    cloves, 9 thick orange slices,
    halved

In a slow cooker, stir together cider, juices and brown sugar; add cinnamon sticks and cloves. If desired, push additional cloves into rinds of orange slices; add to slow cooker. Cover and cook on low setting for 2 to 3 hours, until hot; stir again. Discard spices at serving time. Makes 18 servings.

Look for small muslin drawstring bags at shops where loose tea is sold...they're just right for enclosing whole spices in slow-cooker beverages.

Hot Apricot Cider

Cindy Neel
Gooseberry Patch

Some spring days are almost as cool as late fall! When the breezes are blowing, this warm beverage will take the chill off.

4-1/2 c. apricot nectar
1/4 c. lemon juice
2 c. water

1/3 c. sugar
1/4 t. ground cloves
4 3-inch cinnamon sticks

In a slow cooker, combine juices, water, sugar and cloves; stir well. Add cinnamon sticks. Cover and cook on low setting for 2 to 3 hours, stirring after one hour. Stir again before serving. Makes 8 to 10 servings.

Hosting a ladies' luncheon? Impress your guests with a yummy slow-cooker brie! Add a round of brie cheese to a slow cooker, and top with 1/3 cup chopped candied pecans and 1/4 cup chopped dried cranberries. Cover and cook on low setting for 4 hours, or on high setting for 2 hours. Serve with sliced apples, slices of crusty bread or crisp crackers.

S'Mores Fondue

Annette Ingram
Grand Rapids, MI

*I tried this ooey-gooey sweet dip one weekend when my girlfriends
and I were getting together. It's even better than making s'mores
over a campfire!*

14-oz. can sweetened condensed
   milk
1/2 c. caramel topping
2 t. allspice

1 lb. melting chocolate, chopped
1/4 c. dark chocolate chips
graham crackers, cookies,
   marshmallows

Combine condensed milk, caramel topping and spice in a 3-quart slow
cooker; stir well. Add chocolates. Cover and cook on low setting for
1-1/2 hours, or until melted. Stir well until smooth. Serve with graham
crackers, cookies and marshmallows. Makes 8 servings.

Insert skewer sticks in large marshmallows to swirl & twirl in
sweet caramel or chocolate fondue. Choose marshmallows
in pastel colors for even more dipping fun!

Spice-Coated Pecans

Carol Davis
Edmond, OK

We have an abundance of fresh pecans from our trees and this is such a great gift item. Sometimes I'll coat the finished clusters in melting chocolate...yummy!

1 egg white, beaten
1 t. water
1/4 c. brown sugar, packed
1/4 c. sugar
1 t. cinnamon
1/4 t. nutmeg
1/4 t. allspice
4 c. pecan halves

Spray a 4-quart slow cooker with non-stick vegetable spray; set aside. In a large bowl, beat together egg white and water well. Stir in sugars and spices. Add pecans; turn to coat well and spoon into slow cooker. Cover and cook on low setting for 4 to 4-1/2 hours, stirring once after 2 hours. Spread pecans on non-stick aluminum foil; cool and break into clusters. Store in an airtight container. Makes about 4 cups.

Chocolate Nut Cups

Anne Alesauskas
Minocqua, WI

These sweet nut clusters take me right back to my childhood when I pop one in my mouth. Change them up with walnuts and pecans, or stir in dried cranberries or flaked coconut at the very end.

1 lb. melting chocolate, cut up
2 lbs. white melting chocolate, cut up
3 1-1/2 oz. chocolate candy bars, cut up
32-oz. jar dry-roasted peanuts
16-oz. pkg. whole almonds

In a slow cooker, layer all ingredients in order given. Cover and cook on high setting for 45 minutes without stirring. Turn slow cooker to low setting; stir. Cover and cook for one more hour, or until chocolates are melted. Stir very well. Arrange 24 mini muffin cups on a baking sheet. Using 2 spoons, fill cups with chocolate mixture. Cool completely; store in an airtight container. Makes 2 dozen.

Peach Cobbler 1-2-3

Liz Davies
Spanish Fork, UT

This simple dessert using two kinds of peaches is my own recipe.
Only real butter will do!

1/2 c. butter, melted
3 peaches, peeled, pitted and
  sliced
32-oz. can sliced peaches,
  drained
1/3 c. plus 1/4 c. brown sugar,
  packed and divided

1/3 c. plus 1/4 c. sugar, divided
2 t. cinnamon
18-1/2 oz. pkg. yellow cake mix
2 eggs, beaten
1 c. milk
1/2 c. rolled oats, uncooked
1/4 c. all-purpose flour

Spread melted butter in a slow cooker; set aside. In a bowl, combine fresh and canned peaches, 1/3 cup brown sugar, 1/3 cup sugar and cinnamon. Stir well; let stand for 15 minutes. In a separate bowl, combine dry cake mix, eggs and milk; mix well to form a thick batter. Pour batter into slow cooker; spoon peach mixture evenly over batter. In a small bowl, combine oats, flour and remaining sugars. Sprinkle oat mixture over top. Cover and cook on low setting for 3 to 4 hours, until batter is golden around the edges. Serve warm. Makes 6 to 8 servings.

Fresh whipped cream makes any homemade dessert extra special. In a chilled bowl, with chilled beaters, beat one cup whipping cream until soft peaks form. Stir in 2 teaspoons sugar and 2 teaspoons vanilla extract...and enjoy!

Lemon-Poppy Seed Upside-Down Cake

Rogene Rogers
Bemidji, MN

*We love lemon-poppy seed cake and this one makes
its own custard-like topping!*

16-oz. pkg. lemon-poppy seed
   muffin mix
8-oz. container light sour cream
1 egg, beaten

1-1/4 c. water, divided
1/4 c. lemon juice
1/2 c. sugar
1 T. butter

Combine dry muffin mix, sour cream, egg and 1/2 cup water in a bowl.
Stir until well moistened. Spread batter in a lightly greased 3-1/2 quart
slow cooker; set aside. In a small saucepan, combine remaining water
and other ingredients. Bring to a boil over medium-high heat; stir well.
Pour boiling mixture over batter; do not stir. Cover and cook on high
setting for 2 to 2-1/2 hours, until lightly golden around the edges.
Turn off slow cooker; tilt lid so it is slightly ajar. Let cake stand for
about 30 minutes. When cool enough to handle, hold a large plate
over the top of crock; invert crock and turn out cake. Makes 10 to
12 servings.

Create a super cool centerpiece for a dessert party.
Clean an empty ice cream tub, fill with floral foam
and tuck in some bright flowers.

Coconut Rice Pudding

Chantel Bitter
Larose, LA

Garnish this creamy pudding with a sprinkle of pistachio nuts.

1 c. medium-grain rice,
   uncooked
1/2 t. salt
2 14-oz. cans light coconut milk

2-1/2 c. water
2/3 c. sugar
1-1/2 t. vanilla extract
1/2 t. garam masala or nutmeg

Spray a slow cooker with non-stick vegetable spray. Add rice and salt; set aside. Combine coconut milk, water and sugar in a saucepan; bring to a boil over medium heat. Add to slow cooker; stir well. Cover and cook on high setting for about 2 hours, until rice is tender. Stir in vanilla and spice. If pudding is too thin, stir gently until excess liquid is absorbed. If too dry, stir in a little hot water. Serve warm or chilled. Makes 6 to 8 servings.

Bananas Foster

Missy Abbott
Hickory, PA

My family has loved this dessert ever since we first tried it in an upscale restaurant. We longed to taste it again...with this recipe, we can, without all the fuss and expense!

4 bananas, sliced
1/4 c. butter, melted
1 c. brown sugar, packed
1/3 c. spiced rum or apple juice

1 t. vanilla extract
1 t. cinnamon
1/2 c. chopped walnuts
Garnish: vanilla ice cream

Spray a 3-quart slow cooker with non-stick vegetable spray; layer banana slices in the bottom. In a bowl, mix together remaining ingredients except garnish; spoon over bananas. Cover and cook on low setting for 2 to 3 hours. To serve, spoon over scoops of ice cream. Makes 4 to 6 servings.

Tapioca Salad Dessert

Janis Parr
Ontario, Canada

This luscious dessert is rich and creamy...perfect for those times
when you want to treat your family to something special.
It's always a hit with everyone!

2/3 c. large pearl tapioca,
    uncooked
1/2 c. sugar
1/8 t. salt
4 c. water

1 c. seedless grapes, halved
1 c. crushed pineapple, drained
11-oz. can mandarin oranges,
    drained
1 c. whipped cream

Mix together tapioca, sugar, salt and water in a 3-quart slow cooker.
Cover and cook on high setting for 3 hours, or until tapioca pearls are
almost transparent. Cool thoroughly in refrigerator. Just before serving,
stir in fruit and whipped cream. Serve chilled. Makes 10 to 12 servings.

Dessert to go! Spoon sweet treats into mini Mason jars. Add the lid
and tie on a spoon with a ribbon bow. Perfect for sending home
with guests as a gift that says "Thanks for coming."

Black Forest Cake-Cobbler

Mel Chencharick
Julian, PA

When I was given this recipe to try, I didn't believe you could make a cake in a slow cooker. Well, yes you can! It's not exactly a cake, and not quite a cobbler..but it's scrumptious! It combines the taste of chocolate and cherry. A big "thank you" to Christie for this terrific recipe.

1/2 c. butter, melted
8-oz. can crushed pineapple,
    drained and juice reserved
21-oz. can cherry pie filling

18-1/4 oz. pkg. chocolate
    cake mix
Garnish: whipped topping

In a bowl, mix melted butter with reserved pineapple juice; set aside. Spread crushed pineapple evenly in the bottom of a slow cooker. Spoon pie filling evenly over pineapple. Sprinkle dry cake mix over pie filling. Stir butter mixture again; drizzle over cake mix. Cover and cook on low setting for 3 hours. To serve, spoon into dessert bowls; let cool about 5 minutes, as pie filling will be very hot. Garnish with a dollop of whipped topping. Makes 10 servings.

Whip up some homemade cherry pie filling in no time. Just combine one pound pitted tart cherries, 3/4 cup sugar, 1/3 cup cornstarch and 2 tablespoons lemon juice in a saucepan over medium heat. Bring to a boil, then simmer until thickened.

Hot Fudge Peanut Butter Cake

Marsha Baker
Pioneer, OH

This warm, fudgy cake is the ultimate company-worthy dessert!
It's also delicious made with semi-sweet chocolate chips
instead of the peanut butter chips.

1 c. all-purpose flour
1-1/2 c. brown sugar, packed
   and divided
6 T. baking cocoa, divided
2 t. baking powder
1/2 t. salt

1/2 c. milk
2 T. butter, melted
1/2 t. vanilla extract
1-1/2 c. peanut butter chips
1-3/4 c. boiling water
Garnish: vanilla ice cream

Spray a 3-quart slow cooker with non-stick vegetable spray; set aside. In a bowl, combine flour, one cup brown sugar, 3 tablespoons cocoa, baking powder and salt. In a separate bowl, combine milk, butter and vanilla; stir into flour mixture just until combined. Spread batter evenly in slow cooker; sprinkle with peanut butter chips and set aside. In a small bowl, combine remaining brown sugar and baking cocoa; stir in boiling water. Pour over batter; do not stir. Lay 2 paper towels over top of slow cooker before adding lid to catch any moisture. Cover and cook on high setting for about 4 hours, until a toothpick inserted in center comes out clean. Turn off slow cooker; let stand, covered, for 15 minutes before serving. Serve warm, topped with a scoop of ice cream. Makes 6 to 8 servings.

Many slow-cooker recipes can be speeded up by cooking on high for half the time specified on low setting. For best results with slow-cooker baking, though, use the setting that the recipe calls for.

Cran-Apple Cobbler

Lynnette Jones
East Flat Rock, NC

This is a comforting dessert for fall or winter...really, anytime you'd like something sweet and fruity!

1 T. butter, softened
2 Rome or Golden Delicious
   apples, peeled, cored and
   very thinly sliced
1/3 c. brown sugar, packed
3 T. all-purpose flour
1 t. cinnamon

14-oz. can whole-berry
   cranberry sauce
16-1/2 oz. tube refrigerated
   sugar cookie dough, sliced
   1/4-inch thick
Garnish: sugar

Coat the inside of a slow cooker with butter. Arrange apple slices in the bottom; set aside. In a bowl, combine brown sugar, flour, cinnamon and cranberry sauce; spoon over apples. Arrange cookie dough slices on top; sprinkle with sugar. Cover and cook on low setting for 3 to 4 hours, until dough is set. Makes 6 to 8 servings.

Easy Cherry Cobbler

Carol Stepp
Dennison, IL

A quick no-fuss dessert. It tastes great with peach or apple pie filling too. I use it while camping...it can cook while you enjoy yourself!

21-oz. can cherry pie filling
18-1/2 oz. pkg. yellow cake mix

1/2 c. butter, melted
1/3 c. chopped nuts

Spoon pie filling into a slow cooker. Combine dry cake mix and melted butter in a bowl; mix well and sprinkle over pie filling. Sprinkle nuts on top. Cover and cook on low setting for 2 to 3 hours. Serve warm. Serves 4 to 6.

Fruit Dump Cake

Kathy Kehring
Scottsdale, AZ

A scrumptious quick & easy dessert that's always a winner at family get-togethers and potlucks.

15-oz. can crushed pineapple
15-oz. can sliced pears
12-oz. pkg. fresh cranberries
1/2 c. brown sugar, packed
1 t. ground ginger

18-1/2 oz. pkg. yellow cake mix
1/2 c. butter, sliced
Optional: vanilla ice cream or
   whipped cream

Spray a 5-quart slow cooker with non-stick vegetable spray. Layer undrained pineapple, undrained pears and cranberries. Sprinkle with brown sugar, ginger and dry cake mix. Arrange butter on top. Cover and cook on low setting for 3 to 4 hours, until a toothpick inserted in center comes out clean. To serve, scoop into dessert bowls. Serve warm, topped with ice cream or whipped cream, if desired. Makes 12 servings.

Serve ice cream-topped desserts to a party crowd, the quick & easy way! Scoop ice cream ahead of time and freeze in paper muffin liners.

Ritzy Fruit Cobbler

Sue Morrison
Blue Spring, MO

This is an original recipe of mine. It's a very good way
to use up odds & ends of frozen fruit.

4 c. frozen blueberries, cherries,
   blackberries, strawberries,
   raspberries, sliced peaches or
   a mixture, divided
1 c. sugar, divided
1 sleeve round buttery crackers,
   divided

2 T. butter, softened
Optional: cinnamon to taste
juice of 1 lemon
Garnish: vanilla ice cream

Spray a slow cooker with non-stick vegetable spray. Add one cup frozen fruit; sprinkle with 1/4 cup sugar. Arrange 8 whole crackers on top. Continue layering, making 3 more layers of fruit, sugar and crackers. For top layer, crush remaining crackers; mix with butter and remaining sugar. Sprinkle cracker mixture on top; add cinnamon, if desired. Sprinkle with lemon juice. Cover and cook on low setting for one to 1-1/2 hours, until bubbly and fruit is juicy. Stir gently, breaking up crackers; the crackers will thicken the mixture. Serve warm from slow cooker, topped with a scoop of ice cream. Makes 4 to 6 servings.

For calorie-counting friends, fill a party tray with beautiful fresh strawberries and sliced peaches. Add a sweet dip made of 2 cups Greek yogurt, 1/2 cup honey and a dash of cinnamon. Any extra fruit can be tossed into a salad the next day.

Pumpkin Bread Pudding

Kathe Nych
Mercer, PA

Especially good in the autumn and at Thanksgiving...it fills the house with such a delicious pumpkin aroma! It's even great for breakfast. A terrific way to use up stale or leftover bread.

2 to 4 c. bread, cubed
1/4 c. butter, melted
29-oz. can pumpkin
2 c. milk
4 eggs, beaten

1/4 c. sugar
1 t. vanilla extract
1 t. cinnamon
1 t. nutmeg

Coat the inside of a slow cooker with non-stick vegetable spray. Combine bread and melted butter in a bowl; toss to coat. Add enough bread cubes to line slow cooker; set aside. In a separate bowl, beat together remaining ingredients; pour over bread cubes. Cover and cook on high setting for one hour, or on low setting for 3 to 4 hours. Makes 4 to 6 servings.

Bread pudding is a scrumptious way to use up day-old bread. Try French bread, raisin bread or even leftover cinnamon buns or doughnuts for an extra-tasty dessert!

Chocolate-Pumpkin Bread

Pamela McCourt
Marlboro, NY

For ten years, I would make this bread with my first-grade class before Thanksgiving. We'd put the ingredients together in the morning, making sure every child had a chance to help measure, and placed it in the slow cooker. It was ready by snacktime and the whole wing of our school building smelled wonderful!

1 to 2 T. butter, softened	1-1/2 c. sugar
1-2/3 c. all-purpose flour	1/2 c. oil
1 T. pumpkin pie spice	1 c. canned pumpkin
1/4 t. baking powder	1/2 c. water
1 t. baking soda	1 c. semi-sweet chocolate chips
3/4 t. salt	Optional: 1/2 c. toasted nuts
2 eggs, beaten	

Choose a loaf pan or metal coffee can that fits into your slow cooker. Generously coat pan with butter; set aside. In a bowl, mix flour, spice, baking powder, baking soda and salt. In a separate large bowl, beat together eggs, sugar and oil; beat in pumpkin and water. Add flour mixture to egg mixture; stir in chocolate chips and nuts, if using. Spoon batter into pan; place in slow cooker. Cover and cook on high setting for 3 to 4 hours, until a toothpick inserted in center comes out clean. Cool bread in pan 15 minutes. Turn out onto a wire rack; cool completely. This bread freezes well. Makes 12 to 15 servings.

A loaf of homemade bread is always a welcome gift! Make sure it stays fresh and tasty...let the bread cool completely before wrapping well in plastic wrap or aluminum foil.

Grandma's Apple Pie in a Crock
Rochelle Rootes
Saint Francis, MN

I remember the aroma that came from my grandma's kitchen every fall when she made this scrumptious dessert.

8 tart apples, peeled, cored
   and sliced
3/4 c. milk
1/3 c. brown sugar, packed
1-1/4 t. cinnamon
2 eggs, beaten

1/4 t. allspice
1 t. vanilla extract
1/4 t. nutmeg
1 c. biscuit baking mix
3 T. cold butter, sliced

Spray a slow cooker with non-stick vegetable spray. Layer all ingredients in the order listed. Cover and cook on low setting for 6 to 8 hours, until apples are tender and top is golden. Serve warm. Makes 4 to 6 servings.

Create a heavenly glaze for apple desserts. Melt together 1/2 cup butterscotch chips, 2 tablespoons butter and 2 tablespoons whipping cream over low heat.

INDEX

INDEX

Sandwiches

INDEX

Find Gooseberry Patch
wherever you are!

www.gooseberrypatch.com

Call us toll-free at 1·800·854·6673

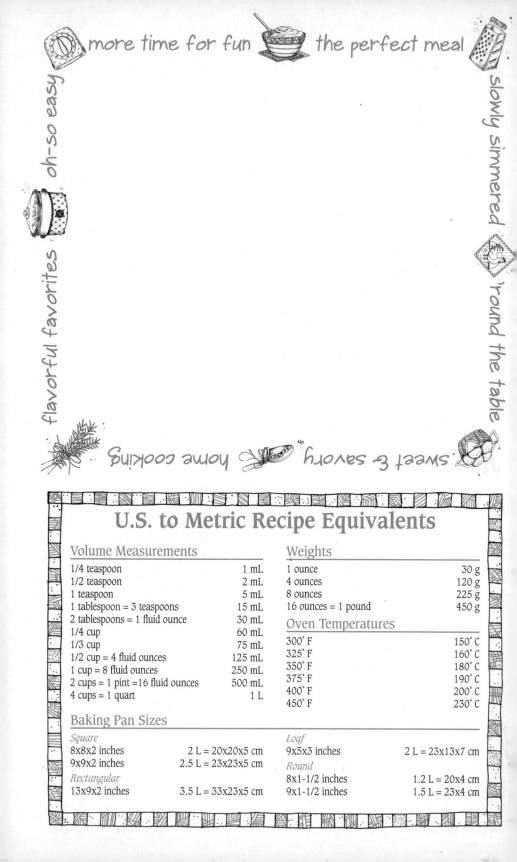

more time for fun   the perfect meal

oh-so easy

slowly simmered

flavorful favorites

'round the table

home cooking   sweet & savory

U.S. to Metric Recipe Equivalents

Volume Measurements

1/4 teaspoon	1 mL
1/2 teaspoon	2 mL
1 teaspoon	5 mL
1 tablespoon = 3 teaspoons	15 mL
2 tablespoons = 1 fluid ounce	30 mL
1/4 cup	60 mL
1/3 cup	75 mL
1/2 cup = 4 fluid ounces	125 mL
1 cup = 8 fluid ounces	250 mL
2 cups = 1 pint =16 fluid ounces	500 mL
4 cups = 1 quart	1 L

Weights

1 ounce	30 g
4 ounces	120 g
8 ounces	225 g
16 ounces = 1 pound	450 g

Oven Temperatures

300° F	150° C
325° F	160° C
350° F	180° C
375° F	190° C
400° F	200° C
450° F	230° C

Baking Pan Sizes

Square	
8x8x2 inches	2 L = 20x20x5 cm
9x9x2 inches	2.5 L = 23x23x5 cm
Rectangular	
13x9x2 inches	3.5 L = 33x23x5 cm

Loaf	
9x5x3 inches	2 L = 23x13x7 cm
Round	
8x1-1/2 inches	1.2 L = 20x4 cm
9x1-1/2 inches	1.5 L = 23x4 cm